COMPUTERS
IN ACTION

COMPUTERS IN ACTION

How Computers Work

SECOND EDITION

DONALD D. SPENCER

Computer Science Consultant

HAYDEN BOOK COMPANY, INC.

Rochelle Park, New Jersey

DEDICATION

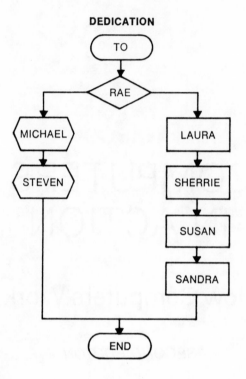

Printed in the United States of America

7   8   9   PRINTING

81 82 83 84 85 86   YEAR

Preface

Computers are having a profound effect on today's society. Our lives not only are influenced by these machines, but in some cases are actually dependent upon them.

Everyone knows that computers exist, but few people know much about them. We read or hear about computers all the time. Newspapers regularly carry articles about them. Television shows mention them frequently. Banks, engineering firms, airlines, hospitals, government offices, the police, industry, utility companies, and the like have all made computers part of their daily routine.

This book was written as a guide for the layman who is attempting to understand computers, for personal computer users, for businessmen who are considering adopting computers, for nonscientific and nonbusiness college students, and for high school students and teachers. It will not teach anyone to be an expert computer programmer, but it will afford some appreciation for the way computers are used in our present society.

The book is short, intentionally so. Most people would not want to read a lengthy book as a first introduction to computing. It is also intended to be readable. Many photographs, diagrams, and cartoons are used to illustrate specific concepts and equipment. Although the computer field is burdened with highly esoteric terminology, I have attempted to keep the technical terms to a minimum and have appended simple, easy-to-understand definitions for many of them.

New features to this edition are:

1. The inclusion of microcomputers and microprocessors.
2. The inclusion of semiconductor memory, magnetic bubble memory, laser memory, ROM, PROM, EPROM, and RAM.
3. The inclusion of new memory devices and concepts, such as floppy disks and virtual memory.
4. The inclusion of new input-output units, such as intelligent terminals, point-of-sale terminals, and COM units.

5. The inclusion of a section on structured programming, the APL language, and the RPG language.
6. New photographs of microcomputer systems, computer applications, input-output devices, and storage devices.

Regardless of one's role in our society, a minimum knowledge of computers is essential. It is my hope that this book will make it easier for everyone to obtain an understanding of this fascinating tool and its social and economic implications.

I wish to thank the computer equipment manufacturers and computer users who supplied me the photographs used in the book. Last, I wish to thank Rae, my chief typist, cook, homemaker, housekeeper, youth advisor, babysitter, and proofreader, who, incidentally, is also my wife.

DONALD D. SPENCER

Ormond Beach, Florida

Contents

COMPUTERS
IN ACTION

1

The Computer Age

Why Are Computers Important?

To many people, a computer is no more than a large box covered with flashing lights; others fancy it as a container with a robot inside; most correctly think of it as a complicated electronic machine that can perform calculations at unimaginable speeds; but some even view it as some sort of super device that will one day control the world. People often ask questions such as the following: Are computers more clever than people? Do they have feelings of love and hate? Can they think for themselves? Can they replace people at performing everyday jobs? Will they eventually make slaves of the human race?

Everyone has come to know something about computers from TV, at the movies, in books, newspapers, and magazines. Probably most of the articles and pictures were rather sensational: Computer Makes a Mistake and Overpays XYZ Company Employees by $2,000,000; Computer Causes the African Bulldogs to Loose Football Championship; Computer Fires Rocket off Target. Cartoonists delight in giving computers almost godlike stature and minds of their own that like to play tricks on ordinary mortals.

It is small wonder that the general public is confused about computers. They don't realize that many of the news items are utter nonsense or in error because of insufficient facts or poor understanding on the part of a journalist. Since the press, TV, and radio are accustomed to stressing the odd or exciting elements in their news in order to capture the attention of their audiences, only sensational stories are apt to receive widespread publicity. As a result, the public is prone to blame computers for the problems that occur in data processing applications.

> **data processing:** the operations performed on *data*—or raw facts—usually by automatic equipment, in order to derive information. There is nothing new or mysterious about this; all of us use data processing every day in

English 171, Section BC
The friendly computer went mad and signed 267 students in this class. We have no choice. The section has been cancelled. There are approximately 55 places available in other sections.

Message written on a blackboard by a university English professor, who blamed a class overload on the computer when it was really just a keypunching error.

just about everything we do. For example, what really happens when you drive your car up to an unfamiliar intersection? The color of the light, a sign on a pole, some lines on a map are all pieces of data that you must process in your mind in order to decide whether to stop, turn, or go straight. Notice that the map, the sign, and the lights are the pieces of data used in the data processing, and that the movement of the car is the result of the information that they supply.

Funk & Wagnall's definition of a computer is as follows:

Computer—*N*   **1.** One who or that which computes. **2.** An electronic machine for the high-speed performance of mathematic and logical operations, or for the processing of large masses of coded information.

That is all there is to it. The computer is basically a very fast calculating machine. What a computer can do, however, and what help it needs from the outside may surprise even the most alert reader.

Many people are afraid of computers because they don't understand them and are always hearing about "computer problems." One of the main purposes of this book is to counteract the *blame the computer syndrome* by emphasizing the important distinction between the computer and the people who manipulate it. The general public must come to recognize the essential role that human choice plays in the successful use of these machines.

Prominent among the products of technology that have shaped our society are automobiles, airplanes, steam engines, electric power, printing presses, radios,

This computer system, located twelve miles from the race site, provides timing analysis and scoring for the Gold cup regatta at a speed of over 8,800 miles per hour compared to the somewhat over 150 miles per hour of the hydroplanes (*Courtesy,* Burroughs Corp.).

television, and telephones. They provide us with transportation, with aids in our physical labor, and with convenient ways to communicate. They have radically altered the pattern of our business and private lives. However, each of these products has also brought society ills, problems, and frustrations.

The computer, another product of technology, is now changing centuries-old ways of doing things and may possibly bring about the greatest social revolution in the whole history of mankind. The most remarkable machine yet invented by man, it is already affecting whole areas of society, opening up vast new possibilities by its extraordinary feats of rapid calculations that multiply by many millions of times some of the capabilities of the human mind. That it should also bring problems and frustrations should surprise no one.

Toward an Understanding of Computers

Most computers of the 1940s were used for scientific computations and were located at government or large university facilities. During the 1960s big business began experimentation and research to determine if computers could handle its routine work. Management was looking for an automated administrative function to produce better reports more quickly, replace clerical employees, perform during employment shortages, and manage a mounting surge of paper-work handling.

In the 1960s computers began to be used in applications not even envisioned in the 1950s. In the 1970s computers started invading the lives of practically everyone—in stores, in hospitals, in businesses, and in the home. Today, small computers are found in common devices such as microwave ovens, sewing machines, automobiles, video game machines, and gas station pumps.

Computer costs range from several million dollars a system to a few hundred dollars. Microcomputer systems (small computer systems) that cost only a few hundred dollars are now available.

A computer is simply an information processing machine. Information goes in and other information comes out, much as dirty clothes go into a washing machine and clean clothes come out. The cleaning process can be thought of as processing. A computer is a machine that processes information or data (data is a term which refers to information that may consist of numbers, words, symbols, or a combination of these). A computer has provisions for storing information internally. This internal storage is called the computer's storage facility or memory. Thus, a large amount of information, say the names and addresses of all the credit customers of a drug store, could be put into a computer, and all that would come out would be an acknowledgment that the information had been stored. Later, when the names and addresses were needed for a mailing list, a short request for this information, put into the computer, would cause all the previously stored names and addresses to be printed out.

The information a computer works with must be objective and precisely expressed. Computers can't work with feelings or subjective ideas unless they are expressed objectively. Neither computer information nor computer results are ambiguous, despite the fact that their meanings aren't always obvious to all people.

All computer information is expressed in a very simple numeric code. Letters, digits, punctuation marks, words, numbers, mathematical signs, sentences, formulas, pictures, sounds, electrical signals: all of these are represented in computer code.

A computer program is a detailed set of instructions for doing a particular job. A program is not usually considered a part of a computer because it doesn't exist physically, just as an idea doesn't. Programs are often called *software,* while the physical components of a computer system are called *hardware.* A computer without a program is about as useful as a pet rock.

A computer can do only a small number of simple processing operations. Its mathematical powers, for instance, may be limited to addition, subtraction, multiplication, and division. If the computer is to accomplish some complex calculation, such as determining the flight path of a spacecraft going to Mars, then the program must break the required calculations down into a series of additions, subtractions, multiplications, and divisions. This program may consist of several thousand instructions.

The most important type of program generally furnished with a computer is a language translator. This program translates between your English language and the computer's machine language so the computer can understand the programs of instructions that you communicate to it. This translator program may be called a compiler, an assembler, or an interpreter. There are several English-like languages that are used to program computers. The short names (acronyms) for some of these languages are BASIC, FORTRAN, COBOL, PL/I, APL, and RPG. These languages are called higher level languages and are widely used for solving all types of problems.

Some of the low cost microcomputers have no language translators, so one must communicate with them in machine language. Although such communication is educational for the person who wishes to understand how a computer works in detail, it isn't an easy language for a person to use.

Most people tend to think of computers as highly expensive, extremely large machines. Some computers do fit this description, but many others do not.

A large scale computer will rent for about $15,000 to $45,000 per month and cost from about $700,000 to $2,000,000. The installation will take up one or more large rooms.

A large computer system, the IBM System/370 Model 165 (*Courtesy,* IBM Corp.).

The IBM System/32 is an easy-to-operate, desk-sized computer developed for computer users in small businesses. The System/32 rents for about $1,000 per month.

A small-scale computer system, the IBM System/32, has features that facilitate its use by persons with no previous data processing knowledge or experience (*Courtesy,* IBM Corp.).

A minicomputer (*Courtesy,* Interdata Corp.).

A minicomputer is to a large-scale computer what a one-story building is to the Sears Tower, or a helicopter is to a 747 jetliner. In other words, minicomputers that cost only a few thousand dollars are well suited to the needs and resources of many schools, small businesses, and others who could never afford more expensive machines.

The IBM 5100 microcomputer being used by business planners to help them solve problems with the company's profits, schedules, and productivity (*Courtesy,* IBM Corp.).

Today, however, there is a very low-cost machine that is being used widely in many application areas. This machine, called a microcomputer, is small and inexpensive enough to be incorporated into other machines. Thus, future machines such as typewriters, television sets, household appliances, pinball machines, automobiles, cash registers, and game machines may have built-in computers. These computerized machines can carry out far more complex instructions than can their present-day counterparts.

Microcomputers may also be used for general applications. These machines, which have been available for only a few years, will have a greater impact on most people and businesses than any other kind of computer discussed in this book.

A white-hot steel slab, which the operators can see through the window, is beginning a trip through the rolling mill, the entire operation under the direction of a computer system that controls all temperatures and speeds (*Courtesy,* General Electric Co.).

What Computers Can Do

The computer is changing the world of business. It has opened new horizons in the fields of science and medicine, improved the efficiency of government, and changed the techniques of education. It has affected military strategy, increased human productivity, made many products less expensive, and greatly lowered the barriers to knowledge.

Computers route long-distance telephone calls, set newspaper type, help design automobiles, navigate ships and airplanes, prepare weather forecasts, check income tax returns, direct city traffic, diagnose human ailments, compose music, play chess, schedule classes, grade test papers, draw pictures, and even help the housewife plan meals.

Computers can store every variety of information accumulated by man and instantly recall it for use. They can calculate tens of millions of times faster than the brain and solve in seconds problems that would take batteries of

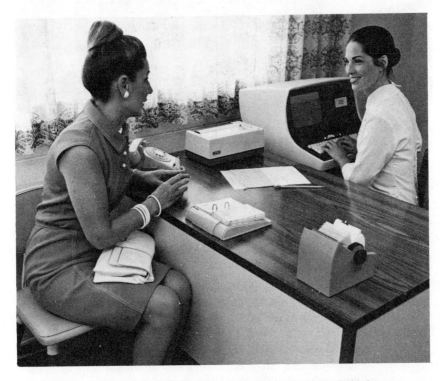

Physicians, nurses, and others requiring information from the medical information system simply identify themselves to one of the display terminals, like the one above, located strategically throughout the hospital. The requesting individual can then perform a wide variety of functions at the terminal: from assigning a bed to a new patient to obtaining the health status of a patient in the intensive care unit (*Courtesy,* NCR Corp.).

The Hawaiian Airline system uses more than 50 display devices such as this one in reservation offices and ticket counters to depict flight information within seconds after requests are made via the display keyboard (*Courtesy,* Sanders Associates, Inc.).

experts years to complete. No one should have to spend long hours adding long columns of numbers, entering accounts in ledgers, keeping inventory records, making out bills or checks. This is all good and proper work for a machine. Beyond such mundane chores, of course, the computer does jobs that could never be done fast enough by unaided human minds. If the computer had not been developed, Neil Armstrong and Edwin Aldrin, American Astronauts, would have been unable to walk on the moon on July 20, 1969. The computer's incredibly rapid calculations and ability to relate information were basic to the lunar landing.

Computers help design other machines (including computers), give them production orders, and then direct their operations. Given adequate data, they can even indicate with high probability the course of a number of things to come.

The dream of the computer-controlled home is now on the verge of reality, and the driving force that will make it possible is the microcomputer.

A computer in every home! It may not be too far away. The minicomputer system shown here can provide a complete home computer center (*Courtesy, Apple Computer Inc.*).

Between January 1975—when *Popular Electronics* magazine published a cover story on the MITS Altair 8800 hobby computer—and January 1977, nearly 25,000 computers found their way into American homes. Today, microcomputer systems are being purchased from manufacturers and computer stores at a rate of several thousand per month.

What is being done with home computers? Most of the first purchasers of home computers were electronic hobbyists who were happy to spend the many hours needed to design, build, test, and fix their new "toy." Today we find people from 5 to 91 using their home computers to regulate the air conditioner, to balance the family budget, to keep track of grocery shopping, to plan menus, and to play video games such as ping pong and space war.

Many of the home computers can be purchased in kit form or already assembled. A kit, like the traditional model airplane, requires time and work to put it together. A computer kit often takes from 50 to 200 hours to assemble; accessory kits generally require less time. Most computing kits require skill and knowledge of electronics.

Clearly, it is only a matter of time before microcomputers will be as much a fixture in the home as the microwave oven, and as common in the small office as the copying machine. Widespread acceptance of home computing awaits only the marketing of a "Volkskomputer" as a general consumer product, at which

Several microcomputers and input-output devices are available in build-it-yourself kit form. Shown here is the Heathkit H11 microcomputer, which is based on the Digital Equipment Corp. L11 microprocessor (*Courtesy*, Heath Co.).

time the image of the home computer will be elevated from its present hobby status to the status of appliance or tool. Like the power hand drill, for example, the home computer will be used by the unskilled for a variety of general purpose tasks as well as by skilled home craftspeople for more creative projects. Home computers are sold by manufacturers, by almost 1,000 computer stores located throughout America and other parts of the world, by mail order electronic equipment companies, and by well-known electronic equipment companies such as Radio Shack and Heathkit. Within the next few years we might expect other major electronic equipment companies such as Lafayette and general retail outlets such as Sears Roebuck and Montgomery Ward to sell home computers.

The computer is more than a prodigy of information and analysis. It never forgets what it has acquired. In time, it will respond to oral command and report in both written and spoken English. Through space satellites and data communications links, technical and other information will one day be instantly available from computer centers around the globe, automatically translated into the language of the user.

What Computers Cannot Do

Of all myths about computers, perhaps the most widespread and in the long run the most dangerous is the one that goes: *computers think for you.* A computer can no more think for you than can a screwdriver or the automobile

The planning and management of the moon's voyages could not have been done without the aid of computers both on the ground and in the spacecraft (*Courtesy*, National Aeronautics and Space administration).

you drive. Indeed, the reactions of a dog to external influences more closely resemble those of a man than those of a computer do; but who would expect his dog to *think* for him?

Although the computer is extremely fast in its calculations, it is absolutely incapable of doing anything but carry out the instructions that have been written for it and placed into it by human beings. It has no more intelligence than a hammer or a rock and is totally useless without human direction.

Can you conceive of a computer inventing its own problems? No, computers do not think and therefore they cannot create their own problems. They can never reproduce or replace the human thinking process. Computers can manipulate and combine items of *data*, but they cannot, beyond the strict limits

Faces on a computer-controlled electric sign scowl their disapproval at a logo-type as part of a series of rhythmic and humorous sequences beamed at passers-by (*Courtesy,* Westinghouse Electric Corp.).

of their instructions (programs), infer any meaning or *information* from this result. Human beings do this with great facility, both consciously and unconsciously.

data: elements or items of knowledge that may be regarded as facts, not necessarily meaningful.

information: knowledge that has meaning to the human mind beyond the data that it contains. For example, the apparently meaningless series of digits, 326432510750, could be called "data." To a payroll clerk, however, to whom the figures mean that employee number 3264 worked 32.5 hours and should be paid $107.50, the series of digits would be "information."

A computer must be instructed (by a computer program) to perform a series of logic and arithmetic operations by a human being who knows the *language* of the computer. The human being, then, is the agency that commands the computer. The computer is his electronic slave, just as the huge elephant working in a tropical forest is the slave of his mahout. The man does the thinking; the computer or the elephant does the work.

computer language: the set of symbols by which a human being communicates instructions and commands to a computer. A computer performs its various functions by means of a series of instructions called a *program.*

The computer is a willing slave and will perform whatever it is instructed to do. However, it will produce a million incorrect answers just as fast and as willingly as it will compute a million correct ones. Human beings must thus exercise great care in preparing instructions for the computer. These must be absolutely unambiguous, precise, and complete to the last detail. If they are not, the computer is very likely to produce "unexpected" answers. Unexpected answers are often mislabeled "creative answers" because they provide information that was previously unknown to the user and thus give the appearance of original thought. All the computer has actually done, however, is to carry out the instructions that were specified beforehand. The reason that the results are a surprise is probably that there were so many calculations to be made or facts to be analyzed that no one could estimate what the outcome would be.

By now the reader should be convinced that certain human functions are indispensable to the operations of computers. It is a human being who must conceive the need for the computer's work, who must prepare the instructions for that work, and who must put the whole process into motion. It is supremely unlikely that computers will ever pose an unmanageable challenge to man. For all his shortcomings, man is uniquely capable of responding to unforeseeable contingencies for which there are neither precedent nor experience. Instinct, intuition, inspiration have raised man to his highest peaks, and mere computer logic will never attain comparable levels.

Can a computer make value judgments by answering such questions as: Is it beautiful? Does it have a fragrant smell? Is it ethical? Such problems are so

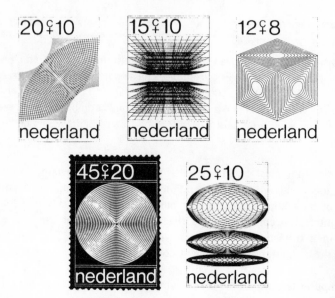

Computer designed stamps produced by the Netherlands General Post Office.

difficult to handle with a computer that those who try must almost always accept unimaginative or severely qualified results. Here then is another of man's irreplaceable roles—the use of wisdom and judgment. A computer may help with such problems by retrieving or processing the applicable data, but a human being must use his common sense and experience to make the decisions.

Human beings (some of them) have imagination and therefore the ability to create the mental image of something new. Numerous attempts have been made to engage computers in various elementary forms of creativity that would seem to duplicate this human faculty. Computers have been programmed to write music, draw pictures, write stories and plays, compose poetry, and design patterns. So far the results have been rather limited. A computer, having no imagination of its own, is entirely dependent on man for the ability to create.

Can Computers Make Mistakes?

Human beings can make mistakes in arithmetic—adding 24 and 7 to get 32, putting a decimal point in the wrong place, multiplying 326 by 4 to get 1204. Human beings also write and copy numbers incorrectly—for example, copying the number 364410 as 364140 or 346410. Human beings make judgment mistakes, filing mistakes, identification mistakes. All of these are *human* mistakes and are not the kind that a computer makes.

A computer performs *exactly* the job that it is instructed to do. However, there may be errors in the computer instructions which will make the computer

"Listen, buster! Without me, you're
nothing, do ya hear, NOTHING!"

appear to make the kind of mistakes listed above. Defects in computer instructions are obviously the fault of the person who prepared them, not of the computer.

Human mistakes have resulted in fouling up billing procedures, payrolls, traffic routing, purchase orders, production orders, and other operations. For example, the computer might be given an order for 50 pairs of shoes, and because of a defect in the program it might cause a purchase order to be printed for 50 *dozen* pair, not being capable of recognizing this as a mistake. Most mistakes of this type can be circumvented by careful preparation of computer instructions, or by correcting the instructions when the error is first detected.

There is another type of human mistake that is called "GIGO" by computer users. "GIGO" stands for "garbage in—garbage out" and is a way of saying that if there is an error in the data fed into a computer, or if those data are incomplete or are in the wrong sequence of presentation, then the computer will *process* them as instructed, all right, but the resulting output—whether a customer bill, a paycheck, an airline seat reservation, an engineering design—will be worse than useless.

"I know my careless programing
resulted in a $10,000 error . . .
but I said I was sorry, didn't I?"

process: a generic term comprehending various operations such as computing, printing data, getting data into the computer, and so forth.

So much for *human mistakes*. Let us now look at some computer mistakes, called *computer malfunctions*. Computers are susceptible to extreme environmental conditions such as electrical disturbances, temperature, humidity, polluted air, salt air, and dust. Computer designers attempt to provide against such conditions, but sometimes computers malfunction when forced to operate under them. (Many computers built for military use are specifically designed to operate in extreme environmental conditions—such as aboard a ship, in a tank, spacecraft, airplane, or missile.)

A computer can malfunction when some foreign electric disturbance takes place that affects the electrical pulses through all its parts. A few extraneous pulses here and there can cause a large amount of trouble that may not be detected immediately. Data transmission *errors* may likewise occur during thunderstorms or solar storms. Such errors cause the data being transmitted to or from a computer to be distorted, thus resulting in incorrect printouts or calculations.

error: the general term referring to any deviation of a computed or a measured quantity from the correct value.

Magnetically stored data are vulnerable also. If a strong magnetic disturbance takes place, it may erase or alter data that have been stored on a *medium*
in the form of magnetic bits.

medium: the physical substance upon which data are recorded—for example, magnetic tape, magnetic disk, punched cards, paper, and the like.

Computational errors can also occur in a computer if the numbers being
manipulated become too large for its capacity, or conversely, too small.

Questions

1. Assuming that each computer installation needs six full-time employees,
   calculate the number of people that will be needed to man all U. S. computer installations in 1980 (assume 400,000 installations).
2. The first electronic computers were used for what applications?
3. What is data processing?
4. What is the distinction between *data* and *information*?
5. List ten applications of computers.
6. Distinguish between hardware and software.
7. Give the short names (acronyms) of three programming languages.
8. Which is the smaller computer: a microcomputer or an IBM System/32?
9. What is a home computer?
10. What is meant by the term *medium*?
11. Discuss one instance where the computer might be used to invade personal
    privacy.
12. Can computers think? Explain.
13. Why are computers necessary to the space exploration program of this
    country?
14. How do you think the Internal Revenue System might use a large com-
    puter system?

2

Computer Evolution

Primitive Calculations

Primitive man used his fingers for counting. He could perform simple addition and subtraction by increasing or reducing the number of fingers he displayed. Ten, the number of fingers on both hands, became the basis for the decimal counting system that has served human beings throughout history. In fact, the word *digit*, which now means any symbol for a number from 0 through 9, originally referred to a man's finger.

The Stone Age man counted with stones, sticks, and shells, and recorded the number of animals he saw during a hunt or the number of sheep in his flock by making notches on sticks, marks in clay or sand, or knots in a rope.

One of the earliest types of devices used to facilitate computations was the Chinese Suan Pan, or *abacus* (ab'-a-cuss), known to have been used around 3000 B.C. In the hands of a skilled operator the abacus can obtain results as fast as a modern desk calculator. Although the abacus has never been widely used in the Western World, it has been an important computational device in such countries as China, Japan, Egypt, Russia, and India for centuries. The Japanese abacus is called the *soroban*. In Russia the abacus is called the *schoty*. Addition and subtraction can be performed on an abacus rather simply, but multiplication and division require complicated mental calculations, mostly to handle the carries from one column to the next.

The next significant step in the history of computing was a set of numbered calculating rods invented by the Scotsman, John Napier, in 1614. The rods, called "Napier's Bones," greatly simplified tedious multiplication problems. Napier also compiled the first table of logarithms, which brought about a revolution in ordinary computing.

Early Mechanical Calculators

In 1630, William Oughtred invented the *slide rule*. The principle behind this device is the fact that two numbers can be multiplied by adding their logarithms.

The abacus, an early calculating device dating to around 3,000 B.C., can perform many calculations, in the hands of a skilled user, as fast as a modern desk calculator (*Courtesy*, IBM Corp.).

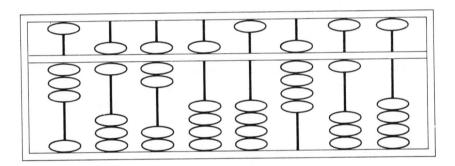

Beads in the smaller compartment of the Japanese abacus, called a *soroban,* have a value of 5 and in the larger, 1, and acquire a counting value when they are pushed against the counting board dividing the two; here the beads are set for a total of 36,750,910.

Thus two rulers may be used with the distance between numbers proportional to their logarithms. By sliding one ruler, multiplication can be rapidly accomplished. Today, the slide rule is still an important calculating device in many professions.

In 1642, only 12 years after the invention of the slide rule, a nineteen-year-old Frenchman, Blaise Pascal, developed the first mechanical calculating machine. This shoe-box size calculator, which was operated with a stylus, took

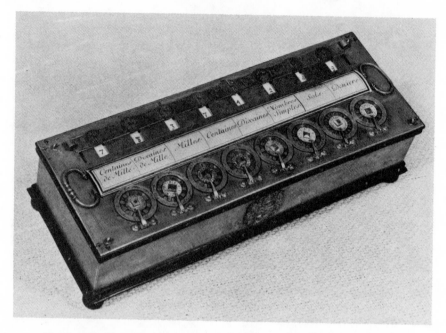

The first practical calculating machine, built in 1642 by the Frenchman, Blaise Pascal, and used to perform addition and subtraction by a built-in automatic means of carrying (*Courtesy,* IBM Corp.).

over the tiresome job of adding long columns of figures. It relied on gear-driven counter wheels to make its computations, and these were used in almost every mechanical calculator for the following three hundred years. His calculator pointed out that a "carry" could be accomplished automatically, that subtraction could be accomplished by reversing the turning of the dials, and that multiplication could be performed by repeated addition. Pascal's machines (several of them were built) worked very well but could perform only addition and subtraction with ease.

Pascal's calculator was improved about fifty years later by the German mathematician, Gottfried Leibnitz. This calculator performed multiplication by repeated addition and division by repeated subtraction; however, like many other machines of this period, it lacked mechanical precision in its construction and was very unreliable and awkward to use.

The Automatic Loom

In 1725, Basile Bouchon designed a simple drawloom for weaving figured silks. The designs in the silks were controlled by patterns of holes punched in a roll of paper. When this "coded" paper was pressed against a row of needles, those which lined up with the holes remained in place; the others moved forward. The loom's action as controlled by these selected needles formed the pattern of the fabric.

In 1728, a French inventor named Falcon designed a loom using punched cards to make various pattern-weaving operations automatic. This technique was later adopted by the first successful machine to operate with punched cards. In 1741, a watchmaker named Jacques de Vaucanson built an automatic loom for weaving figured silks. The designs were established by patterns of holes punched in a metal drum. The holes controlled the selection of threads by raising and lowering the treadles.

In 1801, Joseph Marie Jacquard improved on the ideas of Bouchon, Falcon, and de Vaucanson and built a punched-card loom that has remained basically the same to this day. The Jacquard Loom, which revolutionized the weaving industry, used an endless chain of punched cards that rotated past the needles of the loom. It could weave flower designs or pictures of men and women as easily as other looms could weave plain cloth. A famous portrait of Jacquard himself was produced using 24,000 punched cards.

What Bouchon, Falcon, and Jacquard did with their punched paper and cards was, in essence, to provide an effective means of communicating with the loom. The language was limited to just two "words": *hole* and *no hole*. The same binary, or two-based, system is all but universal in today's machine communication.

Charles Babbage and His Engines

In 1834, Charles Babbage, a mathematician at Cambridge University in England, envisioned a general-purpose machine that would perform arithmetical operations in automatic sequence. This machine, called the *Analytical Engine,* was actually his second calculating device. His first, called the *Difference Engine,* was designed to compute mathematical tables, such as logarithms. Conceived by Babbage in 1812, it was never completed because of financial problems and engineering difficulties. The concept was brilliant, but the assembly of the machine required parts with a then unheard-of precision.

The Analytical Engine was designed to perform complex mathematical calculations and print out the result. This machine, like the Difference Engine, was never built, but Babbage laid the groundwork for modern computers. The Analytical Engine contained all the basic parts of a modern-general purpose digital computer: control, arithmetic/logic unit, memory, input, and output. Babbage proposed to use two types of punched cards to control its operation. *Operation cards* would control the action of the arithmetic unit and specify the kind of operation to be performed, and *variable cards* would control the transfer of numbers (data) to and from the *store*, or memory. Babbage borrowed the

The first modern mathematical machine, the Difference Engine, conceived in 1820 by the Englishman, Charles Babbage (*Courtesy*, IBM Corp.).

punched-card principle from Jacquard's loom. By using these cards it was possible to change the sequence of operations for different problems. Lord Byron's daughter, Lady Ada Lovelace, assisted Babbage in the development of the Analytical Engine and actually designed and refined some of its internal characteristics. She was a brilliant mathematician in her own right and helped to document some of Babbage's efforts. Her development of several programs for performing mathematical calculations on the Analytical Engine surely makes her the world's *first woman programmer*.

The concept of Babbage's Analytical Engine was nothing short of genius, but the engineering problems were overwhelming. It was Babbage's fate to live in an age that did not yet value man's time at its true worth and that had not developed the technology to put his ideas into effect. At his death in 1871, he was remembered chiefly as an elderly eccentric, but his work in mathematics and precision mechanics are recognized today as forerunners of the achievements of contemporary science. Poor Babbage! He was born 100 years too soon. Today, we can appreciate the magnitude of his efforts and the depth of his insight into the principles of calculating machines.

Mechanical Calculators

During the eighteenth century, many attempts were made to improve on the reliability of the machines invented by Pascal and Leibnitz, but the engineering techniques of this period could not produce the precision required. The first machine to perform basic arithmetic operations well enough for commercial use was the *Arithmometer* built by the Charles Zavier Thomas in 1820. Only about 1,500 Thomas machines were actually constructed.

D. D. Parmalee, in 1850, developed a key-driven adding machine that could add a single column of numbers at a time. It was not very reliable and was never manufactured commercially. In 1875, Frank Stephen Baldwin patented the first practical reversible four-process calculator to be invented in the United States. It employed a variant of the Leibnitz wheel—a wheel with a variable number of protruding teeth. W. T. Odhner, a Russian, designed a similar machine in 1878. His calculator used the "Odhner Wheel" developed by Baldwin and made possible the more compact machines that are available today.

In 1884, a bookkeeper named William Seward Burroughs invented the first commercially practical adding-listing machine. Burroughs was born in Rochester, New York, in 1857, and his dream was to develop a machine that would add long columns of figures *accurately*. When he was twenty-seven years old, he succeeded in developing a key-set adding-printing machine with a crank. He formed a company, which later became the Burroughs Corporation, to build the device. Its keyboard and mechanism remain practically unchanged in the Burroughs machine today. Leading mechanical engineers still declare Burrough's principle to be the soundest ever formulated for this purpose.

In 1885, Dorr Felt built an experimental multiple-order key-driven calculating machine with a wooden macaroni box, keys made from meat skewers, key guides made from staples, and rubber bands for springs. In 1887, Felt formed a partnership with Robert Tarrant to produce the *Comptometer*. This calculating machine was so successful that no other comparable machine was placed in competition until 1902.

In 1887, Leon Bollee of France designed the first machine to perform multiplication successfully by a direct method instead of by repeated addition.

Hollerith's tabulating machine, first used to compute the U.S. census in 1890
(*Courtesy,* IBM Corp.).

The device had a multiplying piece consisting of a series of tongued plates representing in relief the ordinary multiplication table up to multiples of 9. The *millionaire,* a popular commercial calculating machine based on the principles developed by Bollee, was manufactured in Switzerland. It required only one turn of the handle for each figure of the multiplier and provided for automatic shift to the next position.

In 1911, Jay R. Monroe, using earlier designs of Frank Baldwin, developed the first keyboard rotary machine to attain commercial success.

Hollerith and the Invention of Punched-Card Machines

It was not until about twenty years after Babbage's death that punched cards were finally applied to data processing. The first punched-card tabulating machine, called the *Census Machine,* was developed by Dr. Herman Hollerith, a statistician, in 1887. Because the population of the United States was growing so fast in the latter half of the nineteenth century, it had been estimated that the results of the 1890 census could not be obtained within the statutory ten years and that there would thus be an overlap with the taking of the next census. To prevent this possibility, Hollerith built a set of machines to reduce the processing time required for the 1890 census.

The 1890 census data were punched in cards by means of a hand-operated punch. A card was punched for each individual in the country. The cards, similar to those Jacquard used, were made the same size as the large dollar bill in use at that time. They were inserted, one at a time, in the Census Machine where the data were tabulated on counters and the cards were sorted. Since the cards could be processed at a rate of 50 to 75 a minute, the 1890 census of 62 million people was completed in only two and one-half years, less than one-third the time needed to complete the 1880 census of 12 million fewer people.

Later Dr. Hollerith organized the Tabulating Machine Company to promote the commercial use of his machines. They were used in many different applications: insurance actuarial work, railroad car accounting, and sales analysis, as well as the 1900 census. Eventually he developed a more automatic card-handling machine, but he was unable to reach an agreement with the Census Bureau for its use in 1910. When his company became too large for individual control, Hollerith sold it, and it later became one of the parents of International Business Machines (IBM) Corporation.

The first automatic calculating machine, the Harvard Mark I, developed in 1944 (*Courtesy*, IBM Corp.).

The Powers Punched-Card System

James Powers, a Census Bureau machine shop expert, developed a punched-card system that was used for the 1910 census. The Powers' machine had 240 keys corresponding to the various possible facts and operated somewhat in the manner of a typewriter or adding machine. All the necessary keys for punching a given card were set before any of the holes were actually punched. This machine increased both the accuracy and the speed of punching. Its success in the 1910 census encouraged Powers to form the Powers Tabulating Machine Company in 1911, the principal competitor for many years of Hollerith's Tabulating Machine Company. Through a series of mergers, this company later became part of the Remington Rand organization, which is now the Sperry Rand Corporation's Univac Division.

Early Electromechanical Machines

Early calculators were basically mechanical devices using gears, levers, pulleys, and the like. Most of them were unreliable, bulky, heavy, and slow. It was inevitable that smaller, lighter, faster, and more reliable machines were soon to be developed. World War II hastened the process because of the need for faster and faster computations. The atom bomb project, for example, required calculations of a complexity never before encountered.

electromechanical: composed of both electrical and mechanical parts.

Several early electromechanical computers were built at Bell Telephone Laboratories, starting in 1938. These special-purpose computers were based initially on the work of Dr. George R. Stibitz. The first of them, called the *Complex Calculator,* is said to be the first computer to employ binary components. This machine, put into operation in 1940, could be remotely controlled and could perform arithmetic operations on two numbers. Models II and III were built to solve military problems and were placed in operation in 1943 and 1944, respectively. Model IV could handle trignometric functions, such as sine and tangent. Model V contained 9,000 relays and 50 pieces of Teletype equipment, weighed 10 tons, and occupied 1,000 square feet of floor space. Model VI, the last of the family, was built for Bell Laboratories' own use and featured many improvements, including magnetic tape storage units.

In 1937, at Harvard University, Howard Aiken began work on an automatic calculating machine called the Mark I. With the help of graduate students and IBM engineers, Professor Aiken's automatic machine was completed in 1944.

The Harvard Mark I was 51 feet long and 8 feet high, contained 760,000 parts, used 500 miles of wire, and weighed about 5 tons. It used a program to

Selective Sequence Electronic Calculator, developed by IBM in 1947 (*Courtesy,* IBM Corp.).

guide it through long series of calculations. It could add, subtract, multiply, divide, compute trigonometric functions, and perform other complicated calculations. Addition and subtraction were accomplished in three-tenths of a second, multiplication in less than 6 seconds, and division in less than 16 seconds.

This pioneering machine, also called the *Automatic Sequence Controlled Calculator,* was put to use during World War II. Allied intelligence discovered that the Nazis were experimenting with an electrically directed cannon. The Mark I was used to evaluate many complex mathematical formulas and resulted in the discovery that such a cannon would never function. While the Nazis continued to waste valuable research time on this project, the Allies were able to ignore it as a military threat.

The Mark I was in operation for more than fifteen years. Compared with modern machines, it was slow and had a very limited storage capacity. It was not

The first electronic digital computer, the ENIAC, developed at the University of Pennsylvania in 1946 (*Courtesy,* Moore School of Electrical Engineering).

a computer such as those we know today. It functioned by means of a wired control panel and made use of concepts found in telephone switching equipment. Nevertheless, it was the first large-scale automatic calculating machine ever to be put in operation.

The Selective Sequence Electronic Calculator (or SSEC) was installed at IBM New York World Headquarters in 1947 and was used through 1952. This machine was 100 times faster than the Harvard Mark I. About the same time, IBM built a machine that could multiply six-digit numbers by counting electronic pulses. This machine, which was simply a tabulating machine connected to some vacuum tubes in a "black box," was known as the IBM 603 electronic multiplier.

Early Electronic Machines

In 1934, Dr. John V. Atanasoff, a professor of physics at Iowa State College (now Iowa State University), modified an IBM punched-card machine to perform calculations mechanically. Five years later, he built a prototype of an electronic digital computer, called the ABC (Atanasoff-Berry Computer). His assistant on this computing machine was Clifford Berry. The ABC, which had a "memory" consisting of 45 vacuum tubes, was assembled in 1942.

In 1946, the Electronic Numerical Integrator And Calculator (ENIAC) went into operation at the Moore School of Electrical Engineering of the University of Pennsylvania. This specialized computer was built to compute firing and ballistic tables to help guide army artillerymen in aiming their guns.

ENIAC, invented by two researchers at the University of Pennsylvania—Dr. John W. Mauchly and J. Presper Eckert—occupied a space of 139.95 square meters (1,500 square feet), weighed about 30 tons, contained about 19,000 vacuum tubes, and required 130 kilowatts of power. The computing elements consisted of many components linked by about a million hand-soldered connections. The input-output system consisted of modified IBM card readers and punches. ENIAC had a limited storage capacity for only twenty ten-digit numbers. (It took 12 vacuum tubes to store one decimal digit.) ENIAC could perform 5,000 additions or 300 multiplications per second. ENIAC, by today's standards, is relatively slow; however, in 1946, the only other machine that could even compete was the ASCC relay calculator that could perform ten additions per second. Needless to say, ENIAC made all relay calculators obsolete.

> **vacuum tube:** electronic circuitry used in all the early electronic computers. Vacuum tubes were replaced with transistors and integrated circuits in later computers.

ENIAC could perform several operations simultaneously, a capability that has only recently become possible with the advent of modern digital computer systems. It could perform several additions, a multiplication and a square root in parallel, as well as solve several independent problems at the same time. It was a fascinating machine that could have been built many years earlier had there been a need for such a machine. Even though there are many amusing stories about ENIAC (stories claiming that all the lights in West Philadelphia would dim when the ENIAC was turned on or that three or more tubes would always burn out when it was started), it was a machine that was so successful that it marked the end of the pioneer stage of automatic computer development. ENIAC was retired from service in 1955.

The Stored Program Computer

In 1945, Dr. John von Neumann recommended in a research report that the binary number system, employing only the digits 0 and 1, be applied in computer design. Dr. von Neumann, one of the world's great mathematicians, pointed out that since electronic components can be in one of only two conditions (on or off, magnetized or not magnetized), these conditions could be used to represent the two binary digits. Dr. von Neumann also proposed that instructions to control the computer, as well as data, should be stored within the computer.

Dr. von Neumann's historic report had a drastic effect on the computing world. ENIAC, the world's first high-speed calculating device had just been developed and, now, at essentially the same time, Dr. von Neumann proposed an entirely new machine. A comparable effect might have been caused if a design of the Boeing 747 had been submitted shortly after the Wright brothers had made a few flights.

The Electronic Delay Storage Automatic Calculator, called EDSAC and built at Cambridge University in 1949, was the first computer to incorporate these ideas. It was no faster in operation than ENIAC, but it did utilize the binary number system and instructions that were stored internally. These instructions were called a *program,* thus the name *stored program.* A similar computer, called EDVAC, was built at the University of Pennsylvania in the early 1950s. It was the second machine designed by the Eckert-Mauchly team.

The Electronic Discrete Variable Automatic Computer (EDVAC) was smaller, more versatile, and more flexible than ENIAC. Although started in 1946, many delays held up its completion until 1952. EDVAC was designed to be a true stored program machine using binary numbers for both instructions and data. Occupying 140 square feet and containing about 5,900 vacuum tubes, it could perform an addition in 864 microseconds and a multiplication in 2.9 milliseconds. Important features of EDVAC have been incorporated in many other machines.

microsecond: one-millionth of a second

millisecond: one-thousandth of a second

Another machine based on the von Neumann report was the IAS computer started at Princeton, New Jersey, in 1946, but not completed until 1952. This machine, developed under the personal direction of von Neumann, was a stored program machine containing 2,300 vacuum tubes. It could perform an addition in 62 microseconds, a multiplication in 720 to 990 microseconds, and a division in 1,100 microseconds. Many machines have been patterned on the IAS computer, among them the ILLIAC (University of Illinois), JOHNIAC (Rand Corporation), MANIAC (Los Alamos), ORDVAC (University of Illinois), and WEIZAC (Weizmann Institute in Israel).

Whirlwind

In 1945, the Massachusetts Institute of Technology was given the assignment to build an aircraft simulator that would simulate flight operation. This project resulted in the construction of a computer called Whirlwind. Designed subsequently to the IAS machine, Whirlwind was completed in 1951.

real time: time as it relates to actual physical processes. For computations to be considered as taking place in real time, they must proceed rapidly enough to allow the results to be useful in the control of physical processes.

Whirlwind was probably the first computer designed with eventual *real-time* applications in mind. Its development was sponsored by the Office of Naval Research and the United States Air Force. Containing around 5,000 vacuum tubes, it could perform over 300,000 additions and 60,000 multiplications per second. Whirlwind proved to be a reliable machine, and many of the ideas it embodied are found in most modern computers. The most important was its *magnetic core* memory, now used as the main memory on almost all computers.

magnetic core: a doughnut-shaped ring of metal which is capable of assuming two states and can thus represent either **binary digit** of some item of data—0 or 1.

Univac I—The First Commercial Computer

The Univac I (Universal Automatic Computer) was the first computer offered as a commercial product. The original model was installed at the U.S. Census Bureau in 1951 and kept in operation for over twelve years. The Univac I was also the first business data processing machine, installed in Louisville, Kentucky at General Electric.

The first general-purpose commercial computer, the Univac I, developed in 1951 (*Courtesy,* Univac Div., Sperry Rand Corp.).

Univac I was developed by Eckert and Mauchly, who had founded their own company before their EDVAC was completed (it later became the computer division of the Sperry Rand Corporation). A direct descendant of their machines, Univac I contained about 5,000 vacuum tubes and was considerably smaller than ENIAC. It could add in 2 microseconds and multiply in 10 microseconds.

Prior to the development of Univac I, input of data to a computer was accomplished by means of punched cards or punched paper tape. Computers so fed spent most of their time reading cards or tapes and printing reports rather than performing calculations. Univac I introduced a much faster way of getting data into and out of a computer—magnetic tape.

Forty-eight UNIVAC I machines were built, and during the early 1950s it was the most powerful device available for solving data processing problems. The machine received a large amount of publicity in 1952 when it correctly pre-

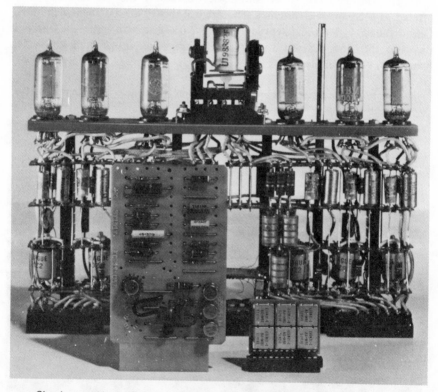

Circuitry used in the first three generations of computers: the vacuum tubes of the first generation (background), the circuit board with transistors of the second generation (left foreground), and the Microminiature components of the third generation (right foreground) (*Courtesy,* IBM Corp.).

dicted the victory of Dwight D. Eisenhower in the presidential election on the basis of incomplete early returns. Not long after UNIVAC I became operational, techniques were developed to improve its usefulness. These techniques have since become the programming languages that are used extensively in solving problems on modern computers.

Early IBM Computers

Shortly after the Korean War started, IBM announced its development of the Defense Calculator, a large-scale scientific computer designed specifically to perform calculations of all kinds. The Defense Calculator, a machine much faster than Univac I, was renamed the IBM 701, and the first unit was delivered in early 1953. It could handle 33 instructions and perform over 16,000 additions per second.

The IBM 650 was the most popular computer in the late 1950s. Development on this machine began in 1949, and the first unit was installed in 1954. After that, over 1,000 machines were placed in service.

In 1955, IBM introduced the IBM 702, the first large-scale computer designed for business purposes. The 702 weighed 24,600 pounds and contained approximately 5,000 vacuum tubes. Althought it could perform over 43,000 additions per second, the 702, like other early computers when compared with modern machines, was something of an electronic tin lizzie. It required tons of air conditioning to keep the room cool where it was installed. Actually, only a few of these computers were ever installed. As soon as IBM announced a newer, more powerful machine, the IBM 705, the 702 was withdrawn from the market—an obsolete machine before it was delivered.

The IBM 704, first offered in 1956, achieved a near monopoly for IBM in the large-scale scientific computer field. It could handle 91 instructions, add in 24 microseconds, and perform either a multiplication or division in 240 microseconds.

Recent Developments

The period from 1954 to 1959 was one of great expansion in the computer field. Many new designs were developed during this period, but nearly all were based on the use of the vacuum tube. Most of the computers built after 1959 used *transistor* circuitry instead.

transistor: a solid-state electronic device which performs the same functions as the vacuum tube. It was developed by Bell Laboratories in 1948. Compared to the vacuum tube, it is smaller, less expensive, requires less power, and generates less heat.

Medium-size computer system of the early 1970s, the NCR Centruy 300 (*Courtesy,* National Cash Register Co.).

Thimble containing 50,000 microminiature components, each of which is equivalent to one transistor (*Courtesy,* IBM Corp.).

The use of transistors greatly increased computer reliability. These devices are not only relatively trouble-free as compared with vacuum tubes, they also increased the speed of most early computers by a factor of 1,000.

In 1959, IBM introduced the 1401 series of computers that dominated the business world until 1964. About the same time it introduced a computer designed for small-scale scientific computations (IBM 1620).

In 1964, a major development in computer design philosophy occurred with the introduction of the IBM System/360 computer. This system satisfied the following computer user needs:

1. The ability to process both scientific and business problems within the same computer system
2. Compatibility of computer systems (that is, programs written for a small computer could now be used by larger computers)
3. Larger storage facilities
4. The ability to communicate with computers via remotely located input-output devices.

The IBM System/360, IBM System/370, and most computers made during the late 1960s and early 1970s utilized *microminiature circuits.*

microminiature circuit: a miniscule circuit in which all the components are chemically formed upon a single piece of material. A typical circuit contains the equivalent of hundreds or even thousands of transistors and other components.

Minicomputers, Microcomputers, and Microprocessors

A *minicomputer* is a relatively inexpensive computer introduced by Digital Equipment Corporation during the mid-1960s. Minicomputers have been designed for use in a wide variety of applications. The typical minicomputer has a purchase price of several thousand dollars, is small (often the size of a small suitcase), is built for simple installation, and does not require a closely controlled environment. It can be maintained by the user, and if it is provided with a user-oriented software system, it can be programmed and operated by people who are not computer experts. In the late 1960s and early 1970s a number of manufacturers got into the minicomputer business, so that now the prospective purchaser has a wide range of models to choose from.

minicomputer: a low-cost computer that was introduced in 1965. Minicomputers are used in business, schools, industry, hospitals, and countless other areas.

A minicomputer system consisting of several magnetic tape units and CRT display units (*Courtesy,* Data General Corp.).

In the mid-1970s Intel Corporation introduced several *microprocessors,* large-scale integration chips containing the calculating and control elements for a computer. Microprocessors are used in video game machines, hand-held calculators, sewing machines, point-of-sale terminals (cash registers), microwave ovens, automobile ignition systems, phototypesetting machines, gas station pumps, slot machines, paint mixing machines, and as control units for a countless number of other devices.

microprocessor: a large-scale integration (LSI) central processing unit contained on a chip. The microprocessor can accomplish processing functions for a wide variety of devices. It is also the heart of a microcomputer.

The first *microcomputer* (Altair 8800) was introduced by MITS in early 1975 (a description of this machine appeared in the January 1975 issue of *Popular Electronics*). The Altair 8800 microcomputer was based on the Intel 8080 microprocessor. The introduction of the Altair 8800 was the beginning of the present wave of personal computers.

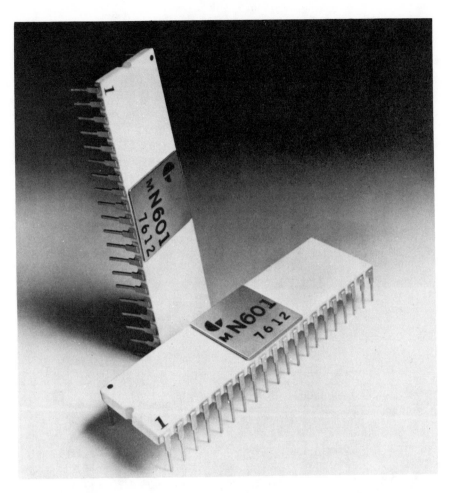

A microprocessor chip. This chip can be used to control many different devices including a microcomputer (*Courtesy,* Data General Corp.).

microcomputer: A small, low-cost computer. A microcomputer contains at least one microprocessor, memory (ROM, PROM, EPROM, or RAM), and input-output circuitry. It functions much the same way as a mini-computer.

Today, microcomputers are being manufactured on a 6.4 millimeter (1/4-inch) square silicon chip (called a *computer-on-a-chip*). Most microcomputers, however, consist of a microprocessor chip, memory chips, and input-output circuitry. Microcomputer technology is still new and new developments are

The Altair 8800b microcomputer. This machine used the Intel 8080 microprocessor (*Courtesy,* MITS Inc.).

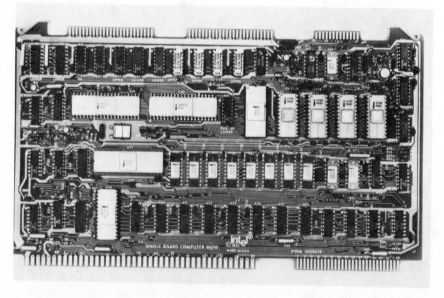

A single-board Intel SBC 80/10 microcomputer that uses an Intel 8080A microprocessor (*Courtesy,* Intel Corp.).

occurring almost weekly. It is impossible to estimate the future growth of the microcomputer industry or the impact of these small, low-cost machines on our society.

Questions

1. The decimal system of counting originated with man's use of (a) knots in a rope, (b) the fingers of both hands, (c) the abacus, or (d) ten stones and a stick?
2. The abacus was developed in what country?
3. An early mechanism for adding and subtracting, using geared wheels, was developed by what Frenchman?
4. In 1834, Charles Babbage designed a machine that contained all the parts of a modern computer. What was the name of this machine?
5. Who built an automatic loom using punched cards that revolutionized the weaving industry?
6. Who invented the first mechanical calculating machine that could perform multiplication and addition?
7. A partly electronic, partly mechanical computer developed at Harvard University was known by what name?
8. When was the first successful digital computer completed? By what name was it known?
9. In what contribution to the computational field did each of the following men participate: (a) John Mauchly, (b) Herman Hollerith, (c) Charles Babbage, and (d) Howard Aiken?
10. What disadvantages did vacuum tube computers have compared with computers using transistors or integrated circuits?
11. The punched cards developed by Herman Hollerith were first used in what application?
12. One of the greatest advances in computing came when the stored-program concept was introduced. (a) Who introduced this idea? (b) In what year was it introduced? (c) What was the name of the first computer that used the stored-program concept? (d) Do modern-day computers still use the stored-program concept?
13. Most of the early computers used what type of circuitry? (a) Vacuum tubes, (b) magnetic cores, (c) wires, or (d) punched cards.
14. What is the name of the first electronic digital computer? When was it invented? Who invented it? Where was it developed?
15. What is the name of the first commercial data processing machine?
16. What was the name of the first computer to use magnetic cores as storage?
17. What was the name of the first computer to use magnetic tape as an input-output medium?

18. Define the following: (a) vacuum tube, (b) transistor, and (c) micro-
    miniature circuit.
19. Most modern computers use what type of circuitry? Why is this circuitry an
    improvement over the vacuum tube?
20. Miniaturization of computer components results in (a) little change in
    computer operation, (b) less reliable computers, (c) much faster computer
21. Who developed the first minicomputer?
22. Explain the difference between a minicomputer and a microprocessor.
23. List five devices that are controlled by microprocessors.
24. The microprocessor was introduced by IBM in 1964. True or false?
25. What is the name of the first microcomputer?
26. How do you think microcomputers will be used in the future?

3

How Computers Work

What Is a Computer?

In the broadest sense, a computer is a device that can accept information, process it, and produce meaningful results. This definition is not very limiting, however, because it covers not only the largest computer but also the clerk in a supermarket. There are two basic types of modern electric computers: *analog* computers and *digital* computers.

An *analog computer* is a type of machine that uses numbers to represent continuously variable quantities that can be measured, such as resistances, voltages, rotations, and the like. Therefore, the analog computer is actually a measuring device. By means of meters, wheels, and gauges the analog computer can measure and process physical variables such as amounts of pressure, temperature, speed of sound, and electric current. A familiar example would be the speedometer on the dashboard of an automobile. The rotations of the car wheels are transferred through a flexible cable to an internal governor device under the dashboard. This device then interprets the rate of speed of the car as revealed by the rotations in terms of a miles-per-hour dial reading.

Another common example of an analog device is the slide rule. The precision of analog devices depends not only on the device but on the ability to read the final results. In the case of the slide rule, it is difficult to enter information into a short rule with accuracy. Likewise, it is difficult to read the results accurately. The longer the rule, the easier is the task of entering information and reading out more accurate answers. Analog computers are used primarily in scientific research and simulation work.

analog computer: a computer in which representation and operations are carried out in analog form, that is, using continuously variable physical quantities.

digital computer: a computer capable of performing calculations on data represented in digital form.

The most distinguishing characteristic of the analog computer is the *continuous* nature of its problem solving. Physical phenomena are simulated by electrical or electronic analogs. These are interconnected in such a way that all phenomena affecting a physical system are simulated electronically, together with the effects they have on all other parts of the system.

To illustrate by means of an example, consider a gun mounted on top of a hill. At a certain time the gun is fired. The path of the projectile is affected by several factors including the angle of gun elevation, the force of gravity, temperature, shape of the projectile, wind direction and velocity, the type and quantity of propellant used in the gun, the altitude of the gun, and the condition of the gun's barrel. All of these factors can be represented by electronic means. In the analog computer the various electronic analogies are interconnected in such a way that virtually any desired item of information concerning the projectile's flight can be computed. For example, it may be of interest to know how high the projectile rises before starting its descent. Or it may be important to know how far the projectile will travel for various angles of gun elevation and propellant charge. The analog computer does not produce numbers, as the digital computer does, but usually produces its results in the form of graphs. In the gun example, the analog computer might produce a plotter trace of a curve corresponding to the path of the projectile.

A *digital computer*, of which the abacus and the adding machine were early examples, works with numbers or letters of the alphabet and special symbols that can be represented by numbers. It solves problems electronically by adding, subtracting, multiplying, dividing, counting, moving, and comparing data. Numerical data can be stored in digital computers until a result is desired. Digital computers are versatile machines and may be used to solve a huge variety of problems. Since most of the computers in use today are digital computers, this book will limit itself to discussing them in subsequent material.

An aura of mystery has come to surround digital computers in the minds of many persons not closely associated with these machines. Fiction writers, journalists, and cartoonists have found a limitless field for their imaginations to create fearsome devices that appear to surpass human beings in intelligence. Fortunately, computers in real life are much less romantic and more understandable. While the large and more sophisticated computers are extremely complex in design and operation, the basic elements of all computers have important similarities. It is not necessary to understand the complexities of the computer's electronic circuitry to be able to use it, any more than it is necessary to understand the construction of the internal combustion engine in order to drive an automobile. For this reason we will leave the lore of computer circuitry to

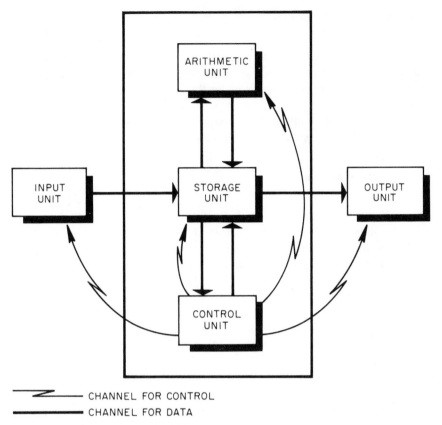

CHANNEL FOR CONTROL
CHANNEL FOR DATA

All computers are composed of the five logical parts shown here.

computer designers and concentrate on some of the ways computers can be used to solve problems.

Digital Computer Organization

Although digital computers come in many shapes and sizes, they are all similar in many ways. Each computer must be able to *read in* instructions and data, *remember* the problem being solved and the data to use, *perform calculations* (and other manipulations) on the data, *read out* the results, and *control* the entire operation. Thus, for a machine to process data it must contain five logical elements:

1. A means of input
2. A means of output
3. An arithmetic unit

4. A means of storing data
5. A control unit.

The five logical elements all work together in solving a problem, and numerical data and instructions are constantly being sent back and forth between them. This entire process is under the control of instructions as specified in a *program.*

Input to the computer may consist of any type of data: commercial, scientific, engineering, statistical, and so on.

Central Processing Unit

The *central processing unit,* sometimes called the *central processor* or *CPU,* is the heart of the computer system. It consists of three logical parts: the arithmetic unit, the storage unit, and the control unit. The central processing unit is often called, simply, the *computer.*

> **central processing unit:** the nerve center of any digital computer system. It coordinates and controls the activities of all the other parts of the computer, and performs all the arithmetic and logical processes to be applied to data. It is convenient to consider the central processing unit as three separate sections: arithmetic unit, storage unit, and control unit. The term is synonymous with **central processor** and **CPU.**

The *arithmetic unit* performs all the arithmetic required by the computer program, that is, the four basic operations of addition, subtraction, multiplication, and division. These four operations are used in a variety of ways to perform other calculations. The arithmetic unit can also perform logical operations such as comparing two items of data for alphabetical, or other, sequence.

The *storage unit* stores the program and data while they are being worked with. The program and data are inserted into the storage area, often called the *memory,* through the input unit. While the computer is solving a problem, the program instructions and data might continually pass back and forth between the arithmetic unit, the control unit, and the storage unit. After the program is finished, the processed data would be transferred from the computer through the output unit. Various forms of computer storage are discussed in Chapter 5.

The *control unit* performs the most vital function in the computer. It directs the overall functioning of the other units and controls the data flow between them during the process of solving a problem. The control unit in turn is controlled by the program; in other words, it merely performs the instructions as specified in the program. Thus a *computer program* is a set of instructions telling the computer what to do. These instructions must be assembled in a logical manner to do a specific job.

computer program: a set of instructions composed for solving a given problem by computer.

Input Devices

An *input device* is a machine that can read previously recorded data from punched cards, magnetic-ink character printing, punched paper tape, magnetic tape, printed documents, voice recognition devices, and other forms. These input devices are an integral part of a computer system and operate under the control of the central processing unit as directed by the computer program. As data are read by the input device's sensing mechanism, they are converted through electronic pulses to magnetic recorded form. Input devices are discussed in the next chapter.

read: to obtain (data) from some source, as, for instance, a storage device. The operation is known as "reading."

write: to record data or to deliver data to a storage device, for example, to punch data on cards in the form of a pattern of holes. The operation is known as "writing."

Output Devices

An *output device* is a machine that reports information from computer storage in a form that can be understood by human beings or that is suitable for use as input in another computer system. Commonly used output devices are typewriters, printers, card punches, display devices, paper tape punches, magnetic tape units, magnetic disk units, and audio response units. Instructions in the computer program may select a specific output device. Output devices are discussed in the next chapter.

input and output devices: machines that provide a vehicle for communication between the computer and the people who are concerned with its operation or between computers themselves. Together they constitute what is known as **peripheral equipment.**

Microcomputers

A microcomputer is a very small but versatile, low-cost, and powerful general-purpose computer that can be programmed to perform specific tasks. Microcomputers are currently being manufactured on a 6.4-millimeter square silicon chip (called a computer-on-a-chip). Most microcomputers, however, consist of a central processing chip (called a microprocessor), memory chips

(ROM, PROM, EPROM, or RAM), and input-output circuitry. A microcomputer system consists of a microcomputer plus application memory, power supplies, control panel, and peripheral units.

A microcomputer (or any other general-purpose digital computer) can perform arithmetic and logic (decision-making) operations and communicate the results to other devices more easily accessible to humans, such as a TV screen, teletypewriter, or audio device. A microcomputer follows commands or instructions (called computer programs) given it by its operator. Connected to memory and input-output devices (peripheral devices) such as printers, cathode ray tube (CRT) display devices, floppy disk memory units, magnetic tape cassette recorders, and teletypewriters, the microcomputer is capable of performing complex tasks such as playing games (tic-tac-toe, backgammon, space war, etc.), computing schedules, creating music, editing text, solving engineering problems, reading X-rays, controlling machinery, and even drawing pictures of Snoopy or Charlie Brown.

A microcomputer will perform any sequence of instructions given to it, even if the sequence is illogical, purposeless, or meaningless—just like a good soldier, it follows orders. Preprogrammed microcomputer software packages and programs are available for certain users (businessmen, noncomputer science

Playing computer games is a popular activity with many microcomputer users. One of the most popular games is space war, based on the TV series "Star Trek" (*Courtesy,* Compucolor Corp.).

teachers, industrial users, etc.) who know little about the interworkings of computers and the techniques involved in using computers to solve problems. Other users, however, find great enjoyment and pleasure in writing application programs in some programming language.

A wide variety of low-cost input-ouput devices has been developed for use with microcomputers: TV displays, keyboard/CRT display devices, teletypewriters, slow-speed printers, magnetic tape cassette units, and floppy disk units.

Microcomputer systems are available from a large number of manufacturers; however, the *neighborhood computer store* seems to be the primary outlet for most of these machines. There are hundreds of computer stores in existence throughout the United States, Canada, and other parts of the world, catering specifically to computer hobbyists, personal computer users, owners of small businesses, and teachers. Most of the computer stores carry a selection of microcomputer hardware and software as well as books, supplies, and other items. Not only will the computer stores sell you a microcomputer system, but they will also teach you how to use it, and they will make adjustments and perform maintenance on the equipment (when required).

Many people are comparing the microcomputer explosion to the revolution brought about by the invention of the transistor. Thanks to the plummeting cost of microcomputers, we will all sooner or later feel the impact of the microcomputer—at school, work, home, and play. It is impossible to list the many different ways microcomputers will be used in the future, for each new day unfolds new uses and applications.

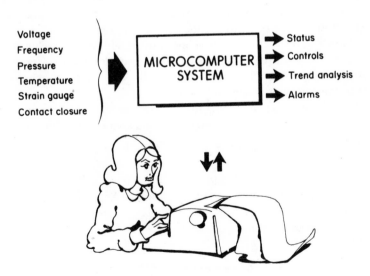

Human-Machine Interaction

A typical job performed by a microcomputer.

How the Computer Works

In Chapter 1 we spoke of the computer as a piece of machinery to be used as a tool. However, most other tools are easier to use; it is usually possible to install them, read the instructions, start them, and get promptly to work. It is not possible simply to push a computer's "start" switch, however, and have it perform useful work. A newly installed computer might be compared (at best) to a five-year-old child, for a child is at first capable of doing very little, but he can by degrees be taught to do a variety of useful things. The more a child is taught, the more complex the work he can do. The computer can also be taught to do many things, but only by a process involving considerable planning, effort, and time. The "teaching" of a computer must be done through the form of programs. Because the computer can respond only to a basic set of simple instructions, problems for it must be broken down into a great number of detailed steps.

The following analogy will help the reader understand the extent to which problems for computer solution must be broken down. Suppose that you wanted to add two numbers, say 36 and 41. This operation certainly sounds simple enough. However, let us examine the thought process required to perform it. First you must determine that you are going to add two numbers. Do you know how to add? If not, you must learn before proceeding. Next you must obtain the numbers to be added. If they are unavailable, then you cannot add. Write down the first number. Write down the second number. Are the numbers aligned correctly? If not, then erase the second number and rewrite it. Repeat this process until the numbers are aligned properly. Then draw a line below the numbers. You are now ready to add the numbers to compute the sum.

This set of instructions for a simple written addition is roughly analogous to the program of instructions which must be provided for a computer. Every process, no matter how elementary, must be broken down into simple-minded steps that the computer understands.

A simplified program might, for example, be the finding of the value of $Y = X^2 + 6$ if X is equal to 4. The program would contain the following steps:

1. Place the value associated with X and the number 6 into computer storage.
2. Bring the value of X from the storage unit into the arithmetic unit.
3. Multiply the value of X by itself, thus forming X^2.
4. Add the number 6 to the product obtained in step 3.
5. Print the answer obtained in step 4.
6. Stop.

This program, written in a language that the computer understands, would originally be read into computer storage via the input unit, step by step, in the same order. After all of the program was in the storage unit, the computer would

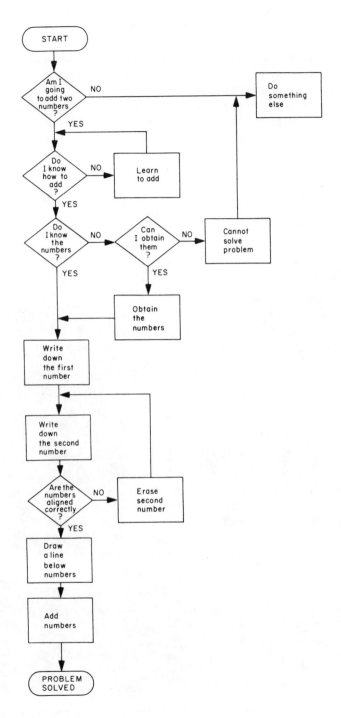

Thought process involved in adding two numbers must be broken down into many simple-minded steps before a computer can be used for the solution.

start processing the program in the following order: step 1, then step 2, and so forth, until the sixth step was reached. At this time the problem will have been solved and the result printed.

The writing of computer programs will be discussed in more detail in Chapters 6, 7, and 8.

Computer Consoles

A computer console is a device that permits the computer operator to communicate with the computer. The console is equipped with a control panel

Control console, including a typewriter, display lights, and switches, used to monitor a medium-size computer system (*Courtesy,* Univac Div., Sperry Rand Corp.).

containing display lights, switches, control buttons and keys, which enable the operator to start or stop the computer as well as send it instructions and data.

Computer consoles are used to monitor and control processing operations being carried out by a computer. Some consoles are equipped with a typewriter in addition to the control panel. The operator can tell what processing is being worked on by the computer by watching the lights on the control panel and reading status messages printed on the typewriter.

Data Representation

The importance of symbols in our civilization lies not in the symbols themselves but in what can be done with them. They may be used to convey information from one person to another. The most common way of representing information to be conveyed is to use a set of symbols. In the English language, these are the familiar letters of the alphabet, numbers, and punctuation marks. The symbols are printed on paper in some predetermined sequence and conveyed to another person by whom they are read and understood.

Communication with a computer system is similar in many ways to communicating with another person as the information to be conveyed must be

Common symbols of communication.

BINARY SYMBOL	0	1
MAGNETIC CORE		
LIGHT BULB		
PUNCHED CARD		
PUNCHED PAPER TAPE		
ELECTRIC PULSE		
SWITCH		

Computer systems use elements that have two states: on or off, magnetized or nonmagnetized, open or closed, punched or unpunched, pulse present or absent.

represented as a set of symbols that can be used by the computer equipment. This set of symbols becomes a communication language between people and machines.

Information to be used as input for computer systems can be recorded on punched cards, punched paper tape, magnetic tape, magnetic disks, magnetic-ink character printing, and optically recognizable character printing. (Other media such as magnetic drums and magnetic cards are most commonly used for computer storage.) Data are represented on punched cards and paper tape by the presence or absence of holes; on magnetic tape and disk, they appear as patterns of small magnetized areas. Magnetic ink characters are printed on paper with a special black magnetic ink that can be read by both human beings and machines. Similarly, characters can be printed on paper and can be read by both human beings and optical reading machines.

Data represented on a recording medium are read into a computer by an input device. This device converts the recorded information into an electronic form that is suitable for use by the computer. Output devices are used to convert information from the computer into punched cards, magnetic tape, paper tape, printed forms, display devices, or audio devices. Information recorded on one medium can be transcribed to another medium by the computer for use with a

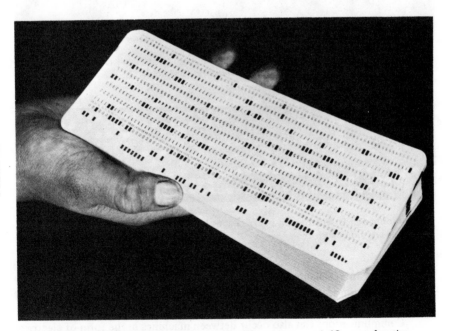

Popular type of punched card having 80 columns and 12 rows for the representation of data (*Courtesy,* IBM Corp.).

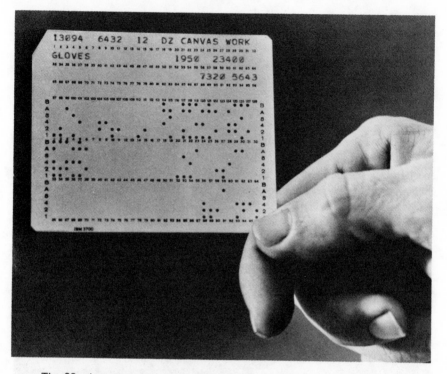

The 96-column punched card, which, although much smaller, can contain more data than the 80-column card (*Courtesy,* IBM Corp.).

Information is recorded on paper tape as holes punched in rows across the tape width (1 inch).

different system; for example, information on punched cards can be recorded on magnetic tape or information on magnetic tape can be converted to printed reports.

Communications can also occur between machines in the form of electrical pulses over telephone wires, cables, or radio waves. The output of one computer system may also be used as input to another machine.

Data within the computer are represented by electrical components: magnetic cores, transistors, integrated circuits, wires, or vacuum tubes. The flow and storage of data through these components take the form of electrical pulses. The presence or absence of these pulses is the method of representing data. For example, a magnetic core can be magnetized in either of two directions and can thus be used to indicate one of two possible states (on or off, one or zero, yes or no) much as the punched or unpunched hole in the punched card is used to represent the presence or absence of like information.

Data-Recording Media

Punched cards are widely used for getting information into and out of computers. Originally developed by Dr. Herman Hollerith in 1887, as we have seen, they have since been used in many different sizes with many different coding schemes. The two most popular types of cards in present use with computers are the 80-column card and the 96-column card.

The 80-column card is 3 1/4 inches wide, 7 3/8 inches long, and contains 12 rows and 80 columns. Information is recorded in the card by rectangular holes (up to 12 x 80, or 960 holes per card) punched in appropriate rows and columns in various arrangements. Cards may be of any color and may have a corner partly cut off to facilitate manual identification. A card may be pre-printed in any manner since the printing is ignored in computer reading operations.

The 96-column card, introduced by IBM in 1970 for the System/3 computer, is capable of holding 20 percent more information than the 80-column card and allows four lines of type to be printed on the card face.

The most serious drawback in using punched cards as an input and output medium for computers has been the relatively slow speed of the card reading and punching equipment as compared to the internal speed of the computer itself. With some equipment, for example, the former might be forty times slower.

Punched paper tape is a widely used medium for computer input. It has also been used for many years as an input and output medium for telegraphic equipment. More recently, it has been used to record information as a by-product of document preparation or checking just as the operation of an adding machine, cash register, or the like can create a punched tape of the data processed. Combining document preparation with the creation of a machine-readable medium can often reduce the costs of preparing data for entry into a computer system.

Paper tape comes in several sizes, but for computer use it is usually 1 inch wide. It is handled either in reels of some twenty to a few hundred feet in length or in short strips of only a few feet. Information is recorded in the form of holes

```
      0123456789  ABCDEFGHIJKLMNOPQRSTUVWXYZ  &·¤-$*/,%/@
Check { C   ||| |   ||   ||| |   ||    | ||   | || |   | ||  |    ||
Zone  { B        |||||||||||||||||||       ||||||
        A        |||||||||        |||||||| |||      |||
        8   |       ||        ||        ||       || || || ||||
Numerical{ 4        ||||      ||||       ||||    ||||     | | | |
        2   | ||  ||    || ||      || ||    || ||      | | | |
        1   | | |  | | |  | | | | | | |  | | | | |  | |  | ||| |
```

Representation of magnetic tape, which is ½-inch wide and comes in reels of
2,400 feet (*Courtesy,* IBM Corp.).

1234567890

Check using characters designed for magnetic ink character reading.

punched in rows across the tape width. Generally, each row represents one
alphabetic character or numeric digit and there are ten rows per inch of tape
length.

Punched paper tape has certain advantages over punched cards as a
computer input medium. The most important is that punched paper tape *records*
are not limited in length and can be as long or as short as desired. With punched
cards, on the other hand, the entire card must be read even if only one or two
columns are needed to record the data, and extra cards must be used if the data
takes up more than 80 or 96 columns. Also, punched tape can sometimes be
produced more quickly and less expensively than punched cards. Both the tapes
and the tape-producing equipment require less space than punched cards and
card-producing equipment.

record: a group of related data treated as a unit.

Punched paper tape also has certain disadvantages as a computer input
medium. Once data are punched into paper tape, it is difficult to correct errors.
Moreover, they cannot be manipulated as data on separate cards can be.

Paper tape input devices can be faster or slower than punched card devices,
depending on the operation being performed. For example, a card reader with a

rated speed of 800 cards per minute can read cards with 80 columns at a rate of 1,067 characters per second, cards with 40 columns at a rate of 533 characters per second, and cards with 20 columns at a rate of 267 characters per second. A fast paper tape reader can read 1,000 characters per second. Thus, a choice between the two media is more complex than a comparison of rated speeds alone would indicate.

Magnetic tape is a principal input-output recording medium for computer systems. Magnetic tape provides a rapid way of entering data into a computer system and an equally fast method of recording processed data from the system. Information is recorded on magnetic tape as magnetized spots called *bits*. The recording can be retained indefinitely, or the recorded information can be automatically erased and the tape reused many times.

bit: an abbreviation for binary digit, one of the two digits, 0 and 1. The term is extended to the actual representation of a binary digit in different forms, for example, a magnetized spot on a recording surface.

So that magnetic tape can be easily handled and processed, it is wound on individual reels or placed in cassettes. The most commonly used tape is ½ inch wide and is supplied in reels of 2,400 feet. A full reel weighs about 4 pounds and can contain information equivalent to 400,000 fully punched cards. (The tape unit can read these data at a rate approximating 300,000 characters per second.) A ¼-inch tape is used in tape cassettes. Data are recorded in parallel *tracks* across the length of the tape. There are seven or nine tracks on the ½-inch tape and one track on the ¼-inch tape.

track: a channel on a magnetic storage device for recording data.

The *magnetic ink characters* that MICR (Magnetic Ink Character Recognition) devices can read were developed by the American Bankers Association in cooperation with the MICR equipment manufacturers. The character set comprises the ten standard numerals plus four special symbols used in check processing: the dash, used in account numbers; the amount symbol, which indicates the beginning of the amount field; the ABA transit routing symbol, which indicates the beginning of the numerical code of the drawee bank; and the on-us symbol, which is put on a check only by the drawee bank and marks off a field used for internal accounting codes.

MICR characters are printed on paper with a magnetic ink. The ink looks like a normal black ink, but it contains a very finely ground magnetic material and a binder to make the magnetic particles adhere to the paper.

Several devices have been built that can read a variety of marks and characters printed on paper. At present, the size, type font, quality of printing, and positioning of characters on the source document must meet several standards before the data can be read reliably by *optical scanning devices.*

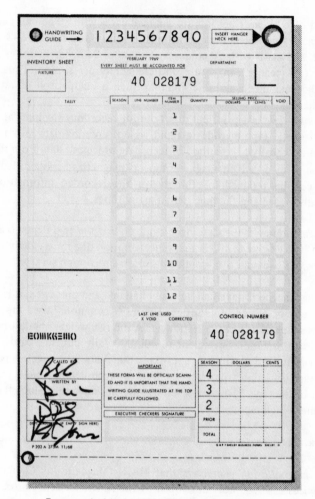

Form used with the IBM 1287 Optical Reader.

optical scanning: a technique for machine recognition of printed characters by the configuration of their images.

Data Preparation

A variety of devices is used to record data from a source document onto a medium suitable for input to a computer system. These devices are not connected to the computer but are used merely to produce the machine-readable input data. The routine of translating raw source data into machine-readable form often involves keypunching information from forms, orders, records, and other source documents into punched cards, punched paper tape, or onto

Data recorded on this form by marks made with a No. 2 pencil or black pen is read directly into a computer via an optical scanning device.

magnetic tape or disks. It may also be transcribed by typewriter for processing in an optical character reader or printed for use with magnetic-ink character equipment.

> **source document:** an original document that is accepted directly into the computer or from which data is prepared in a form acceptable to the computer.

The *keypunch* is a unit that is used to punch information into cards. An operator presses a key on the keypunch, and it punches the appropriate hole or holes in a specific card column. A printing/punch would also print the character, in the same column, at the top of the card.

Several devices are used to punch information into paper tape: type-writers, adding machines, bookkeeping machines, and cash registers.

Some punching units simply punch the tape while other units punch the tape and also produce a readable copy of the information being punched. A unit of this type is the teletypewriter with attached paper tape reader and punch. This machine will produce a punched paper tape containing all keyboard operations in coded form.

> **keypunch:** a keyboard-operated machine used for punching data manual-ly into punched cards.

The reading of punched cards and of paper tape are both relatively slow processes. The conversion of data from a slow input medium to a faster medium can be accomplished by feeding the cards or tape into a converter which reads the slower medium and records the data on a faster input form such as magnetic tape. The magnetically recorded data are then available for high-speed input into the computer system. Several manufacturers make equipment for converting practically any type of machine-readable record to practically any other type of machine-readable record. This includes the conversion of punched cards to magnetic tape or disk, paper tape to magnetic tape, magnetic tape to punched cards.

There are also devices that will record keyed data on standard 2,400 foot reels of magnetic tape, on magnetic tape cassettes, and on magnetic disk packs. These devices are usually called key-to-tape or key-to-disk data entry stations.

Questions

1. What are the two major classifications of electronic computers?
2. A common analog device is the (a) abacus, (b) slide rule, (c) Napier's bones, (d) typewriter.
3. A digital computer performs its computations by (a) analogy, (b) deduction, (c) counting, (d) none of the above.
4. What are the five major units of a digital computer? Give a brief description of each one.
5. What functions are performed by the central processing unit?
6. What is the function of the input unit? The output unit?
7. What is the purpose of the computer console?
8. What is a computer program?
9. Name four media that are used to input information to a computer.
10. What is the name of the machine used to prepare punched cards for computer use?

4

Getting Information In and Out
of the Computer

Introduction to Input-Output Devices

From the last chapter, we learned what elements make up a digital computer system. Input and output devices (often called I/O devices) act as the eyes, ears, and voice of the computer. They provide a method of getting data in and out of computer storage. It is also through the input devices that programs are supplied to the computer. Input devices can be typewriters, punched card readers, magnetic disk units, punched paper tape readers, magnetic tape units, optical scanning devices, magnetic ink character readers, mark sense readers, and other devices.

Output equipment is used to record or display the problem results or information relating to the problem being solved. Common output devices are line printers, display devices, magnetic tape units, magnetic disk units, digital plotters, typewriters, card punches, paper tape punches, microfilm units, audio response units, and other devices.

From the beginning, input and output equipment has acted as a restraining factor on the high speed of the computer. Since most of the data which a computer uses or produces must go through input-output equipment, it is understandable that there is much concern over the speed of these devices. The relatively slow speed of devices such as card readers and paper tape readers is why many systems use magnetic tape and removeable magnetic disks as the primary method of communicating with the computer. Data can be recorded on magnetic tape or magnetic disk by using special data preparation equipment or even a smaller computer system dedicated to this purpose. Likewise, computer output can be recorded on magnetic tape or disk and later transcribed to printed sheets or other forms by the suitable equipment.

Input and output devices are machines connected directly to the central processor and operate under its control as directed by the stored computer program. Reading takes place as the input medium physically moves through an

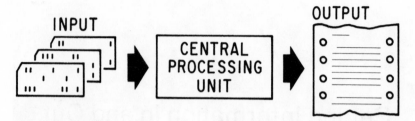

INPUT DEVICES

CARD READER

PAPER TAPE READER

TYPEWRITER

MAGNETIC TAPE

REMOVABLE MAGNETIC DISK

OPTICAL CHARACTER READER

LIGHT PEN

MARK SENSE READER

GRAPHIC TABLET

MICROFILM READER

MAGNETIC INK CHARACTER READER

OPTICAL MARK READER

VOICE RECOGNITION UNIT

OUTPUT DEVICES

CARD PUNCH

PAPER TAPE PUNCH

TYPEWRITER

MAGNETIC TAPE

REMOVABLE MAGNETIC DISK

DISPLAY DEVICE

MICROFILM RECORDER

AUDIO RESPONSE UNIT

DIGITAL PLOTTER

Input/output devices are used to get data in and out of the computer, the former to present the problem, the latter to record the results.

input device. Information is sensed or read and, once converted to a form usable by the computer, is then transmitted to storage. Writing involves converting data from storage to a form or language compatible with the output medium and then recording the data using an output device.

Most input-output devices are automatic; once started, they continue to operate as directed by the stored program. Instructions in the program select the required device, direct it to read or write, and indicate the computer storage location that data will be put into or taken from.

This chapter briefly describes most of the common input-output units that are used with computers. Since magnetic tape and magnetic disks are used not only as input-output but also as a type of computer storage, they and their associated units are discussed in the next chapter.

IBM System/370 Model 165 computer system, including the following input/ output units: eight magnetic-tape units, four line printers, two card readers, computer console, and magnetic-disk storage system (*Courtesy,* IBM Corp.).

Card Readers

Practically every computer can accept data from punched cards, either directly via a card reader or by means of a magnetic tape unit if the punched card information has been copied onto magnetic tape by a machine called a card-to-tape converter.

Data recorded on punched cards can be processed and organized in a number of ways before it is introduced into the computer. Punched card machines can sort cards into any desired sequence; interfile them with other cards; add, subtract, multiply, or divide numeric data recorded on them; print out any part of this data; and manipulate the cards and the data in many other ways.

The *card reader* is a device which reads information from punched cards that have been placed in its *input hopper* and converts these data into an electronic form. After being read, the cards are then carried onto a *stacker* for removal by an operator. There are two types of card reading units in general use: the reading brush and the photoelectric cell.

In the *brush type reader,* cards are mechanically moved from a card hopper through the card feed unit, under reading brushes. The reading brushes mechanically sense the presence or absence of holes in each column of the card. This sensing results in the conversion of the information of the card to electrical impulses that are utilized by the card reader circuitry and stored as data. After the cards have been read they are moved from the card feed unit and placed in the card stacker in the same sequence in which they were fed into the reader.

The *photoelectric type reader* performs the same functions as the brush type; the difference is in the method of sensing the holes. Photoelectric cells are

Card reader (*Courtesy,* Walter Reed Army Medical Center).

Data recorded as punched holes in a roll of paper tape are read as the tape
feeds past the reading head and then translated to electrical pulses acceptable
to the computer (*Courtesy,* Hewlett-Packard).

activated by the presence of light. As the punched card is passed over a light
source in the card reader, light passing through the punched holes activates
photoelectric cells, one cell for each column of the card.

The speed of card reading varies according to the type of reader used and ranges from a hundred or so to several thousand cards per minute.

Paper Tape Readers

Paper tape is adaptable for many applications: scientific data processing, data communications, source data recording, data acquisition, and so forth. The *paper tape reader* works similarly to the card reader. It moves the previously punched tape past a reading unit where the presence or absence of holes in the tape is sensed and converted to electronic impulses acceptable to the computer. Paper tape readers are characterized by their reading methods: mechanical readers detect the presence of holes by mechanical means, while photoelectric readers detect holes by light-sensitive elements. Of the two, mechanical readers are slower but less expensive.

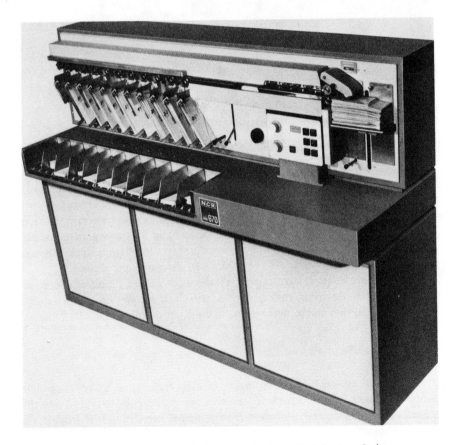

Magnetic ink character reader (*Courtesy,* National Cash Register Co.).

Optical character reader (*Courtesy,* Control Data Corp.).

Mechanical readers operate by passing the surface of the tape over heads consisting of .pins or brushes which close contacts as the heads are passed over holes. One detriment of mechanical readers is that they cause wear on the tape, limiting paper tape life to several hundred passes. Use of a special metal-coated tape, called *mylar,* however, reduces the wear problem to insignificance. Mechanical readers have speeds of up to several hundred characters per second.

Photoelectric readers are capable of speeds of up to a thousand characters per second. Besides being faster, photoelectric readers are also more reliable because they have no mechanical sensors to wear out or jam.

Magnetic Ink Readers

Magnetic ink character recognition (MICR) *readers* can detect characters printed in magnetic ink on paper documents and convert the data read into the proper code for a central processor. The principal users of MICR readers are banks, although other industries, particularly those engaged in consumer credit, have shown some interest in the equipment. All manufacturers of MICR equipment have adopted the specifications for document size and type font set down by the American Bankers Association.

MICR readers were designed originally to process bank checks rapidly, and the document sizes which MICR readers will accept are therefore based on the dimensions of ordinary bank checks. An MICR reader can transmit data read from magnetically encoded documents into the computer. It can also sort the documents into separate pockets on the basis of the data read, either under control of the computer or of the reader itself. It has a feed hopper for input documents, a reading mechanism, and two or more output pockets.

Optical Character Readers

An *optical character reader* (OCR) is a device that will read and transmit data from a printed page directly into a computer. The data to be read by an optical reader are usually composed of upper-case letters, numbers, and special characters that have been typed or printed in ordinary ink on documents that can also be read by human beings. The documents are placed in a hopper and then transported into the reader past an optical scanning position where a powerful light and lens enable the machine to distinguish the letters, numbers, and special characters as different patterns of reflected light. These light patterns are converted into electrical pulses for use by the computer.

Optical Mark and Mark Sense Readers

Optical mark and mark sense reading, somewhat simpler than character recognition, are performed by detecting the presence or absence of pencil marks in specified positions on a form. Many areas of data collection can be simplified by using preprinted forms that require only that the user fill in appropriate boxes with pencil marks. Such forms are commonly used for collecting inventory information, conducting a census, recording a public opinion poll, or taking a test. Forms of this type may be read by *optical mark* or *mark sense readers*.

Documents that are to be read by an optical mark reader can be marked with standard lead pencils. Documents read by mark sense readers must be marked with special pencils containing soft and highly conductive leads.

Voice Recognition Units

Voice recognition devices are used to convert audio signals to digital impulses. Input is rather slow if vocal input occurs at the normal speaking rate but is speeded if the spoken words are recorded on magnetic tape or disk, which can transmit them to the computer at a faster rate.

Form representative of the type designed for optical mark readers.

Although there are only a limited number of voice recognition devices now available, they are promising for many applications where a relatively limited number of spoken words will serve adequately for input of data.

Mark sense reader (*Courtesy,* Motorola Instrumentation and Control, Inc.).

Typewriters

There is usually a typewriter or teletypewriter associated with a computer system. Often it is actually part of the computer console. Typewriters provide a suitable means of entering limited quantities of data into the computer. They may also be used to type limited amounts of printed data. Most typewriters or teletypewriters print data at a rate of either 10, 15, or 30 characters per second,

Operator typing data into the storage of an IBM System/360 computer (*Courtesy,* United Aircraft Corp.).

although several of the newer machines fall in the range of 200 to 300 characters per second. The typewriter serves as both an input and output device.

Intelligent Terminals

The term *intelligent terminal* encompasses a number of computer process-ing characteristics that are physically built into, or attached to, the terminal unit. This enables the terminal to perform some functions normally handled by the computer, thus relieving the load on the computer system or data transmission lines. Specifically, the intelligent terminal detects and corrects certain operator errors, relieves the computer of some routine tasks, speeds up processing, and makes information available more easily and quickly.

Intelligent terminals are usually CRT units equipped with a keyboard. They may be connected (interfaced) with a number of other input-output devices, such as card readers, printers, and cassette recorders. The intelligent terminal, coupled with other I/O devices, greatly increases a computer's capability.

An important function of the intelligent terminal is to capture and enter raw source data at the remote location of its origin, such as a sales office, branch office, or mobile office. Since the terminal can be programmed for specific applications, this ensures that entries are made in the proper places in fill-in blanks. Operators always know exactly what is being entered and where entries are to be made through visual verification with the CRT display. Each entry is checked as it is made, and the operator can make corrections before committing data to the computer by simply rekeying the data.

Many of the intelligent terminals use *microcomputers* or microprocessors to control various functions. These micros can be programmed to perform many unique and special functions that may be required for a special application.

Point-of-Sale Terminals

Computer users are starting to realize the potential advantages of capturing data at the source. Some of the benefits of a good data collection system are: reduction of clerical costs; increased accuracy of information because of the elimination of the manual handling and transcribing of data; more effective cost control; and sounder operating decisions by management, because they are getting timely management information, not history.

Useful data must have at least two characteristics: they must be accurate and timely. Neither of these characteristics can be overlooked. The person who is capturing the data should do the fewest number possible of the simplest things possible.

Characteristics of *point-of-sale* systems are: the input device should be installed as close as possible to the point where the data are generated; the device should be easy to operate by the person at that location who is familiar with the characteristics of these data and with the important effect of errors in the data; precoded information should be used when possible; a method of visual verification and correction is desirable.

For a number of years, some cash registers have been equipped with a paper tape punching mechanism to record the facts of each sale when these facts are entered on the machine's keyboard. For example, the sales clerk enters the amount of sale, tax, and other charges and credits if any. The clerk may also

Point-of-sale terminals, such as this one, are being used in many department stores to expand and speed sales floor service to customers (*Courtesy,* NCR Corp.).

enter the stock number and unit quantity of merchandise sold as well as any other data desired. While this is being done, the machine punches a paper tape with the amount and identification of each item. At the end of the day or period, the punched tape is removed from the cash register and placed in a device that records the data from punched paper tape to magnetic tape to feed the day's sales into the computer, which updates the accounts receivable, cash on hand, and stock records, and produces sales analysis reports for the store management.

This semiautomatic method of capturing data is certainly better than complete manual systems; however, there is still much room for improvement. Today, several companies are producing systems that eliminate the manual keying of data (an excellent place for error to creep into a point-of-sale system).

Today, computerized supermarkets throughout the country are becoming rather common. The key to these checkout systems is an optical scanning device which "reads" an identification code placed on each item of merchandise and transmits this information to the store's computer. The computer uses this information to create a perpetual inventory control system.

The code used to identify products is the Universal Product Code, a ten-digit numbering system for identifying items sold by grocery stores. The first five digits in the code identify the manufacturer; the second five digits identify

Computerized checkout systems are used to speed grocery shopping and selling. As grocery items pass over the reading slot, the optical scanning mechanism reads the Universal Product Code data from a symbol affixed to the bottom of each product (*Courtesy,* IBM Corp.).

that manufacturer's product. This ten-digit code is expressed in a symbol as a series of vertical bars that can be understood by computer equipment. This symbol will be printed on most of the 10,000 items sold in a typical supermarket. Upon receiving the code, the computer would immediately match it with product information such as price. It would then relay these data to a cash register where they would be visually displayed to both the customer and the checker. Simultaneously, this price would be printed on the customer's receipt along with the product name.

Placing the price in the store's computer memory eliminates the tedious job of price-marking items and also eliminates checkout errors that occur because of illegible price marks and ring-up mistakes. The store manager can also use the system to check the inventory of any product, to determine sales up to the moment at any checkstand or in any department, to know total sales, and to change prices of products.

We briefly discussed two areas (retail stores and supermarkets) where point-of-sale terminals are used. The capturing of data at its source is commonly referred to as *source data automation.* No additional steps are needed to transcribe the data to computerized form. Point-of-sale terminals, magnetic ink character reading devices (such as those used by banks), optical character reading devices (such as those used by utility companies), and other recognition devices offer the possibility of preparing data only once at the original source and sending these data directly to the computer. There are many application areas that could be drastically improved by using source data automation systems.

The securities industry is typical of areas where source data automation can be of benefit. At least 40,000 terminals of various types are linked to computers for the purpose of transacting securities business. However, the real problem in the securities industry is that most of its transactions are still on manual or, at best, semiautomated systems. The two causes of operational problems are paper and segmentation. The paper certificate is the basic tool for recording and transferring ownership. Segmentation of the industry has caused the development of many self-contained processes. Even where automation has been applied it is not uncommon to end the process with a printout, hand carry the printout to the next segment in the process, and then keypunch the data all over again. What is needed are a device and a method that will allow the data to be captured once and then carried throughout the automated system.

Display Units

The *cathode ray tube* (CRT) *display unit*—an auxiliary that has been associated with computers for the past two decades—is a desk type unit that has a combination of features that allows one to enter as well as display data. The

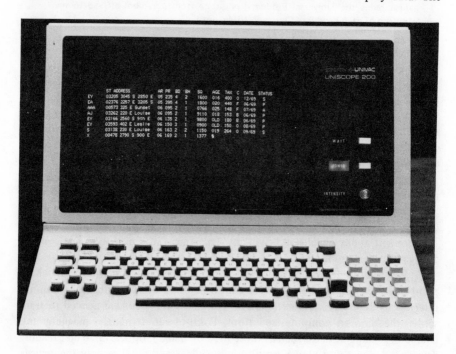

CRT display unit (*Courtesy,* Sperry Univac, a division of Sperry Rand Corp.).

display contains a tube quite similar to the picture tube in a television set. The primary devices that are used to enter data are a light pen or a keyboard.

Typically, the display area on the tube contains about one million points that can be individually controlled. Graphs, lines, charts, tables, letters, numbers, and other figures can be displayed.

A *light pen* is a photosensitive device which detects the presence of light on the display screen. A light pen pointed at the screen will detect light at a discrete time and position and inform the computer. The light pen can be used either to point at information which already appears on the screen or to designate a location at which information is to appear; or it can be used to enter information directly by "printing" characters on the screen.

Several kinds of *keyboards* are often used with CRT units. A keyboard allows the operator to compose messages or make inquiries.

Visual displays are used by businesses to provide easy access to computer-generated information (*Courtesy,* IBM Corp.).

Game paddles or keyboard talk to the Apple II microcomputer that connects to a color television set. This system can be used to play video games, draw color displays, or solve business or scientific problems (*Courtesy,* Apple Computer, Inc.).

Cathode ray tubes are used in airline reservation systems, management information systems, business systems, information retrieval systems, simulation systems, military defense systems, design automation systems, and computer-assisted instruction (CAI) systems. Much work with CRT displays and CAI systems has been done at universities, schools, and research organizations in recent years.

Perhaps the most useful microcomputer output device is a video display unit. A common display unit used with these computers is a TV receiver (a modified home TV unit).

Card Punches

Card punches as a rule are not able to process cards as fast as card readers. Speeds usually average around several hundred cards per minute. The card punch automatically moves blank cards from the card hopper, one at a time, under a

Simultaneous input and output provides a young student with immediate feedback in a Computer-Assisted Instruction (CAI) system (*Courtesy,* IBM Corp.).

punching mechanism that punches rectangular holes corresponding to data received from computer storage. After the card is punched, it is moved to a checking station where the data are read and checked with the information received at the punching station. The card is then moved to the stacker.

Paper Tape Punches

Data from computer storage can be punched in paper, plastic, or metal tape by a paper tape punch. Data are punched into blank tape as it moves through a punching mechanism that punches round holes. Tape punches, being entirely mechanical in nature, are subject to physical restrictions that are similar to mechanical readers. The maximum speed is about 300 characters per second. The slower units are especially desirable for low-speed data collection or off-line data preparation.

Line Printers

The most important output device in a computer system in terms of human legibility is the line printer. A line printer prints a complete line of print

A slow-speed, low-cost printer for use with microcomputers (*Courtesy,* Southwest Technical Products Corp.).

at one time. There are two major categories of printing techniques. In *impact printing,* a type carrier contacts an inked ribbon and paper. In *nonimpact printing,* light-sensitive paper is exposed to a character image to form the printed character. Nonimpact is usually faster than impact printing because of simpler mechanical construction, but impact printing is the more common. Because of the high speeds at which the printing can be accomplished (from 100 to 2,000 lines per minute), a continuous paper is used. The paper may originally be blank, contain lines, or use any preprinted form. The final, computer-printed paper is referred to as *hard copy.*

Line printers are often used for purposes other than printing out numerical answers to problems. In some applications printers are used to produce data in a graphical form. They may also be used to draw flowcharts or pictures.

Slow-speed, low-cost printing devices are being developed for use with microcomputers. One such device is the SWTPC PR-40 line printer. This device prints 64 upper case characters at a rate of 110 characters per second, with 40 characters per line. This printer is available for about $400, or $250 in kit form.

Digital Plotters

A *digital plotter* is a device which can draw graphs and drawings under control of the computer. Typical applications might be the drawings of weather

Line printer producing a continuous sheet of printed matter (*Courtesy,* National Cash Register Co.).

maps, land contour maps, subdivision maps, computerized art, bridge designs, seismic exploration plots, or highway maps.

The two most common forms of plotters are the drum and flatbed types. The pen of a drum plotter is driven in one axis while the paper moves positively or negatively in the other axis. The flatbed plotter moves the pen in both the X and Y axes, and the table is usually fixed.

The central processor provides pen movement and functional commands to the plotter in digital form, and these commands are then automatically converted into pen motions.

Audio Response Units

Audio response units, which generate words via computer linkage with ordinary touch-tone telephones, have been used successfully in banking, manufacturing, and utility applications. An audio terminal permits users to key certain alphabetic and numeric information into the computer system and get computer-compiled spoken responses to their inquiries. The computer's response is heard over the telephone's earpiece.

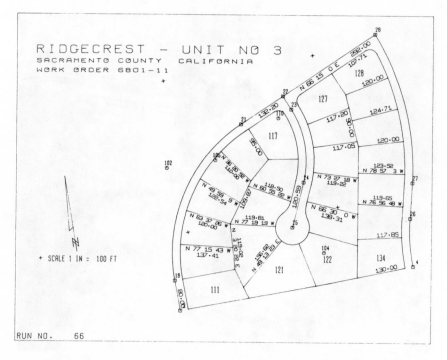

Subdivision map produced by a digital plotter (*Courtesy,* California Computer Products, Inc.).

In audio response systems, the computer is used to recognize the initial contact code, check the input request, plan the response, select the appropriate words from the audio response vocabulary (typically stored on a magnetic drum or disk), and transmit the response.

Although verbal input devices and audio response units are in rather limited use today, it is predicted that great improvements will be made with verbal communication equipment in the future.

Computer Output Microfilm

With the increasing calculating speeds of computers, a growing problem is how to obtain output from the computer. Printers have become faster, but are slow in comparison with the speeds at which computers may generate output.

Computer Output Microfilm (COM) has recently come of age. COM does not solve all problems associated with computer output, but it provides an additional option that system designers may consider.

Instead of printing pages on the printer, the computer generates an output magnetic tape. This magnetic tape is used as input to a COM unit. The COM unit

The KOM-90 microfilm converts output magnetic tapes to 16-millimeter microfilm. Data recording is accomplished at a rate up to 90,000 characters per second (*Courtesy,* Eastman Kodak Co.).

reads data from the magnetic tape, displays them on the face of a cathode ray tube, and photographs them onto 16-millimeter roll microfilm. Data recording is accomplished at a rate up to 120,000 characters per second or 26,000 lines per minute—approximately equal to 300 printout pages per minute.

The COM microfilmer can also be directly connected to the computer (on-line), thus eliminating the necessity of recording the data on magnetic tape.

An alternative to the reel of microfilm is *microfiche,* a 10.16 × 15.24-centimeter (4 × 6-inch) strip of microfilm that contains 208 or more full pages of information. You can make a simple mental comparison of a single, thin microfiche with a stack of hard copy printouts. Microfiche films are simple to file and quick to retrieve. When placed in a microfiche viewer, the single page needed is shown in full size on the screen for easy reading, and, if desired, a full-size photocopy of the single page may be printed out in seconds. Typical output speeds of computer-stored data to microfiche is one microfiche per minute or approximately 12,000 pages per hour.

The uses for computer output microfilm are probably limitless. Microfilm reduces a high volume of documentary data to manageable proportions and frees the user from time-consuming searches and the computer from high-volume printing tasks.

Some fundamental applications of COM are the following:

- Business-oriented listings, with a low or high frequency of reference, but with an infrequent need for updating.
- Computer-generated data bases, such as catalogs, indexes, directories, bibliographies, abstract and financial data.
- Libraries.
- Engineering drawings, including plots, graphs, maps, charts, circuit designs, etc.
- Management information reports requiring both alphameric and graphic output for proper display of data.
- Insurance—examples are agents' commission statements, agents' digest system, positions records, vendors' records, etc.
- Animated movies.
- Educational and training films for industry, hospitals, businesses, government, and schools.

Questions

1. What are the two functions served by input-output units?
2. Why can the computer process data so much faster than input-ouput units can handle it?
3. List five input devices that may be used to input data into a computer.
4. May hand-printed letters and numbers be used as computer input?
5. What is the primary advantage of reading data in the form of magnetic-ink characters? Of optically readable characters?
6. Describe some common business in which optical character recognition equipment might be used.
7. A punched card reader counts the holes punched in each card. True or false?
8. What are some of the main advantages of magnetic tape over punched cards?
9. List four output devices that may be used to output data from a computer.
10. Identify the following abbreviations: (a) MICR, (b) CRT, and (c) OCR.
11. What is the function of a CRT display unit?
12. What are some of the methods of producing computer output as hard copy?
13. Which is the fastest output device, the typewriter or the line printer?
14. What output device would it be best to use if one wanted to draw a picture of Snoopy?
15. Why is printing a most practical form of computer output?
16. What is an intelligent terminal?
17. Explain how and where intelligent terminals are used.

18. What is a point-of-sale terminal?
19. List several areas where point-of-sale terminals might be useful.
20. Explain how the Universal Product Code is used.
21. What is COM?
22. What is microfiche?
23. List several applications where COM equipment might be used.

5

Computer Storage

The capability of a computer to "remember" is one of its fundamental and most essential facilities. It would be impossible for a computer to operate without its having some way of storing instructions, facts, and figures for retrieval when needed. Computer storage is often called *memory*. The memory is actually an electronic file where instructions and data are retained as long as they are required.

When data are placed in storage through an input unit, they remain there until called for by the control unit. Since many computer applications require large amounts of storage, the storage facility of most computer systems is divided into two general types: main storage and auxiliary storage.

main storage: the internal storage of a computer, from which instructions are executed. It is the fastest store of a computer.

auxiliary storage: storage that supplements the main storage, usually supplied by magnetic disks, magnetic drums, magnetic tape, or magnetic cards.

Classification of Storage

Main storage, often called *internal storage* or *primary storage,* is an integral part of the central processor. All data to be processed by the computer must pass through main storage.

Main storage is used to store both instructions and data. The main storage unit must have sufficient storage capacity to hold the program being used and the data needed for the problem. When additional storage is needed, the computer system may be augmented with auxiliary storage.

Auxiliary storage, also called *secondary storage,* is used to supplement the main storage of the computer. Auxiliary storage is of two types: *direct access*

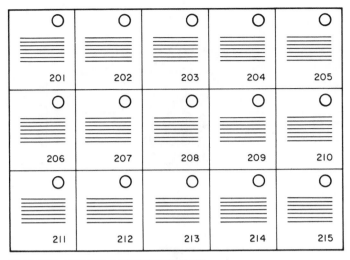

EACH MAIL BOX HAS A UNIQUE ADDRESS

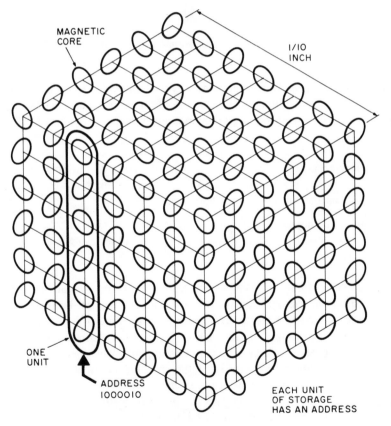

MAGNETIC CORE

1/10 INCH

ONE UNIT

ADDRESS 1000010

EACH UNIT OF STORAGE HAS AN ADDRESS

Main storage of a computer may be compared to a group of numbered post office boxes, each unit of storage having a unique address.

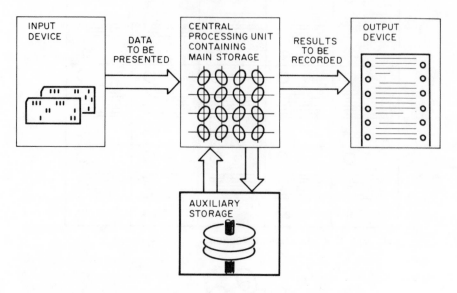

Auxiliary storage is used to supplement the computer's main storage unit.

and *sequential access*. Direct access devices give immediate access to a particular item of stored data. *Sequential access* devices consist of tape units whose stored data must be read *from the beginning* in order to read or write a particular item of data.

direct access: a type of storage in which access can be made directly to the data in any storage location; for example, magnetic core, magnetic disk, magnetic drum, or magnetic card.

sequential access: a type of storage in which data can only be accessed in the sequence in which it is stored in the device; for example, magnetic tape or paper tape.

Auxiliary storage may be used to store both instructions and data. Before these instructions can be executed or these data can be used by the computer, however, they must be brought into the main storage unit of the computer.

Computer programs and data are held in auxiliary storage until called for by the control section of the central processing unit. Whenever this occurs, the control section directs the transfer of the specified information into assigned locations in the main storage. After processing is complete, the same information and processed results can be sent back to the auxiliary storage.

For years magnetic core storage has been the primary type of main storage for computers. Today, however, computer manufacturers are using semiconductor memories in many computers. Almost all microcomputers and minicomputers, and many larger machines use semiconductor memory for their main storage. Auxiliary storage devices include magnetic disks, magnetic tapes, magnetic drums, and data cells.

Storage Addressing

The main storage of a computer can be thought of as resembling numbered mail boxes in a post office. Each mail box is located and identified by its number. In a similar way, main storage is divided into locations, each with a unique *address*. Each location holds a specific unit of data for use by the central processor. A unit of data can be a *digit*, a *character*, a *byte*, a *word*, or a *record*. Each item of data is inserted into or extracted from a specific storage location. Whenever data are inserted into a storage location, they replace the previous contents of that location. When data are extracted from a location, the contents remain unchanged since only a copy of the contents has actually been removed. Once data are placed in storage, therefore, they may be used many times.

address: a number identifying a storage location from which data are to be retrieved or in which data are to be inserted.

byte: eight bits treated as a unit.

word: a set of characters that occupies one storage location and is treated as a unit.

item: a unit of data.

record: a group of logically related items treated as a unit. A file refers to a group of logically related records.

The time needed to locate and transfer data or instructions either to or from storage is called *access time*. The access speed of a computer and the amount of data handled per access have a direct bearing upon the cost and efficiency of the entire system, primarily because the central processor is *constantly* accessing storage for instructions and data as well as replacing new data into storage during the execution of a program. The access time of many modern computers is so rapid that it is measured in billionths of a second, or *nanoseconds*.

access time: the time the computer takes to locate and transfer instructions or data to or from storage.

nanosecond: one billionth of a second (one thousandth of a microsecond).

The *capacity* of a storage device is expressed as the largest number of words, bytes, characters, or bits that it can store at one time. As with access speed, the cost of storage is also greatly influenced by its capacity.

capacity: the maximum amount of data that can be stored.

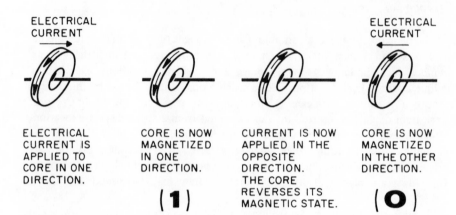

ELECTRICAL
CURRENT

ELECTRICAL
CURRENT IS
APPLIED TO
CORE IN ONE
DIRECTION.

CORE IS NOW
MAGNETIZED
IN ONE
DIRECTION.

(1)

CURRENT IS NOW
APPLIED IN THE
OPPOSITE
DIRECTION.
THE CORE
REVERSES ITS
MAGNETIC STATE.

ELECTRICAL
CURRENT

CORE IS NOW
MAGNETIZED
IN THE OTHER
DIRECTION.

(O)

Principle of the magnetic core.

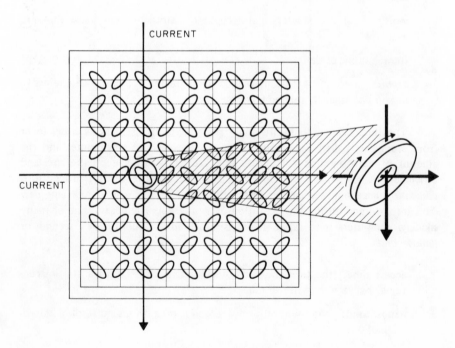

Principle of the core memory plane.

Magnetic Core Storage

A *magnetic core* is a tiny, doughnut-shaped metal ring, a few hundredths of an inch in diameter. Each core is pressed from a mixture of iron oxide powder and other materials and then baked in an oven. It may be magnetized in one direction or the other, the direction of the current determining the polarity or magnetic state of the core. Reversing the direction of current changes the magnetic state. Consequently, the two states can be used to represent the two bits, 0 or 1, plus or minus, yes or no, or on or off conditions. For machine purposes, this is the basis of the binary system of storing information. The core, unless deliberately changed, retains its magnetism indefinitely.

These cores are strung on a grid of wires. In writing bits into storage or reading bits from storage, a particular core is selected by putting electrical signals

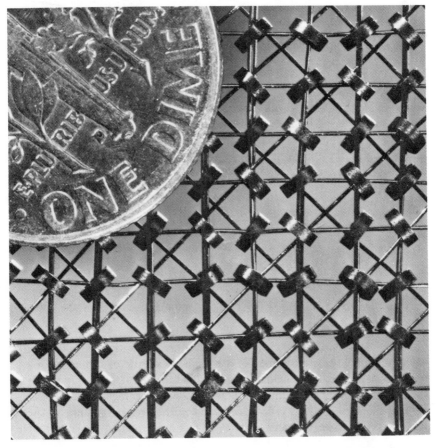

Section of magnetic core memory plane compared in size to a dime (*Courtesy,* General Electric Co.).

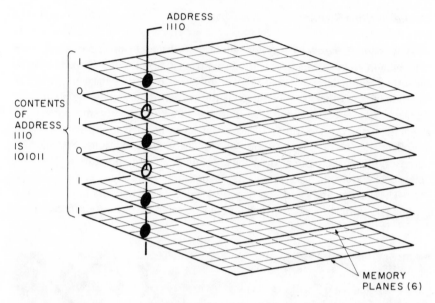

Contents of a single address in a magnetic core matrix.

on the wires which cross at that core. The illustration shows a number of cores strung on a grid of wires. It can be seen that the two wires run through each core at right angles to one another. Half the amount of current needed to magnetize the core is sent through each wire. As a result, only the one core at the intersection of the two wires receives sufficient current to be magnetized; no other core in the arrangement is affected. As a result, many cores may be strung on a grid of wires, yet any specific core can be selected and magnetized without affecting any other.

magnetic core: a small, doughnut-shaped piece of metal oxide capable of magnetically storing one bit.

memory plane: an arrangement of magnetic cores strung on a planar network of wires.

core matrix: the storage unit of a computer composed of several memory planes.

The arrangement of cores shown in this illustration is called a *core memory plane.* The storage unit of a computer consists of a number of such memory planes, each containing several hundred cores. These memory planes are stacked on top of one another as shown in the succeeding illustration. Such a stack of memory planes is called a *core matrix.* Each vertical column of cores in this matrix is assigned an address where one fact or instruction can be stored.

The number of memory planes assigned to a core matrix is a function of the computer size. A memory plane can hold only one bit at each location. To store an 8-bit word, or byte, in one address, we need 8 memory planes. To store a 16-bit word, we need 16 memory planes. To store a 32-bit word, we need 32 memory planes. Each bit of the word is stored on a different memory plane. When writing or reading a word, all the bits in the address are selected simultaneously. For example, in the core matrix illustrated, when the computer reads the contents of address 1110, it will read each of the cores in the column marked 1110, thus providing the stored binary value 101011.

Semiconductor Memory

In third-generation computers, transistors were replaced by integrated circuits, each equivalent to hundreds of transistors. As a result, computers could be made even smaller, less expensive, and more reliable.

In many of the third-generation computers, integrated circuits were also used for high-speed memory, providing some competition for the new long-established magnetic core memory. The integrated circuit memory is called "semiconductor memory," semiconductors being the substances from which transistors and integrated circuits are made.

A *semiconductor memory* uses silicon chips with interconnecting on-off switches (called flip-flops). The direction of the electrical current passing through each cell determines whether the position of the switch is on or off; that is, whether the bit is one or zero. Each silicon chip is about 0.32 square centimeters (one-eighth of an inch square). Semiconductor memories provide increased storage capacity and low access time. It is also possible to design logic into these memories.

Semiconductor memories can be found in many large computers (IBM System/370) as well as in small computers like the IBM System/32, NCR Century 151, and Univac 90/60. Semiconductor memories are used as the internal memory in almost all minicomputers and microcomputers (see following section).

We can expect to see wider use of this type of memory in future systems of all sizes. These memories are both faster and more compact than core memory.

Microcomputer Memory

The most common (and least expensive) kind of microcomputer memory is called RAM (random access memory). It is used primarily to store user pro-

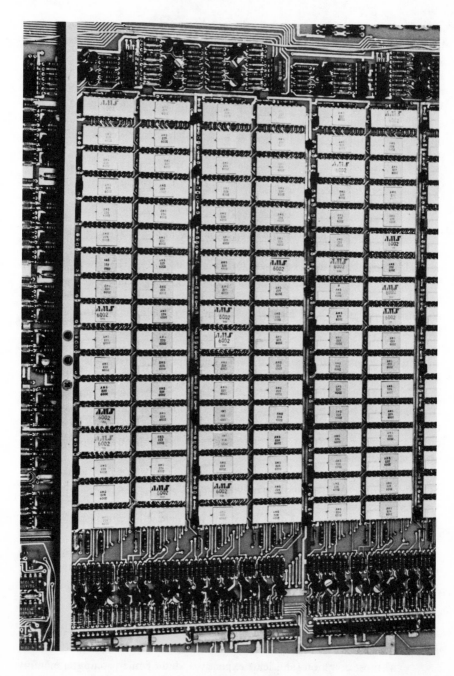

A semiconductor memory board (*Courtesy,* Interdata Corp.).

grams and data; however, the contents are lost when the microcomputer's power is shut off. So a small amount of another kind of memory is needed in the microcomputer: ROM, PROM, or EPROM.

ROM (read only memory) is used to store monitors, interpreters, input-output drivers, or special application programs. It is not possible to write into ROM memory as it is into RAM. ROM memory, however, is not user programmable—the contents of the ROM were put there by the manufacturer. Another memory, called PROM (programmable read only memory), does not forget what it knows when the microcomputer's power is turned off, and is used in many microcomputers to contain monitors, input-output drivers, and special application programs. The PROM chips can be purchased blank and then can be programmed by using a special machine called a PROM programmer or PROM burner. Once programmed, the PROM memory behaves the same as the ROM.

EPROM (erasable PROM) is one of the latest types of monolithic memory. It can be programmed by the user, and it can also be erased and reprogrammed with different information. Once it has been programmed, the EPROM memory acts just the same as ROM. The EPROM is the program memory most frequently used by users who must make frequent changes in their programs. They can do it themselves if they have a PROM programmer.

ROM: Read only memory

PROM: Programmable ROM

EPROM: Erasable PROM

RAM: Random access memory

Bubble Memory

A couple of years ago, IBM announced a bubble memory chip about an inch in diameter, with a ten-megabit (that's one and a quarter million bytes) storage capability. Using such a compact memory you could store the whole Library of Congress in the cubic area taken up by about the average-size console TV set. It should be possible within the next five to ten years to store all the knowledge of mankind in the corner of a classroom.

Bubble memories consist of a thin orthoferrite film in which each "bubble" generated is a cylindrical magnetic domain that carries a polarization opposite to that of the film. Such bubbles, each about 3 microns in size, are packed in densities that go to millions of bubbles per square inch. Ways have been found to move the bubbles stepwise at the rate of at least one million steps a second, and in this fashion, a bubble memory can be used to store data and perform logical operations.

The trouble with bubble memory is that it's accessed serially. This means that each storage cell must be rotated in its entirety to get to any one point. A search through bubble memory is thus serial instead of parallel or random, making access a major stumbling block that must be solved for the full potential of this memory to be realized. The next stage in bubble memory will probably be the development of independent shifts with complex addressing systems, so the information can be accessed through specialized packets.

Presently, bubble memory cannot replace random access memory as the main memory in a computer, because of its slow, serial nature. What it will replace, in its current state, is magnetic disk and magnetic tape.

Disks and tape store data on thin magnetic film. In a disk of tape, though, the film itself moves mechanically at a high speed; in a bubble memory, the bubbles move at high speed through the film. In a disk or tape, the information is fixed in location and passes the read-write head in only one dimension. In a magnetic bubble memory, the information travels in two dimensions anywhere in the film. Bubble memories have an additional advantage. They are able to perform logical operations on stored data without having to read the data back in storage again. Also, bubble memories are electronic and should be very reliable, since they have no moving parts.

In October 1967, the first article on the device applications of magnetic bubbles appeared in the Bell System's technical journal. It was authored by A. H. Bobeck, a frequent contributor to advances in magnetic bubble state-of-the-art. Since that time, magnetic bubble memory development has grown rapidly and will unquestionably continue to do so. Bobeck, still at Bell Laboratories, recently forecast that bubble chips with 10^8 bit capacity should be state-of-the-art by 1985.

Magnetic Tape Storage

Magnetic tape is a triple-threat computer medium since it may be used for input, for output, and for storage. *Magnetic tape units* have provided continuing increases in the speed of data transmission to and from the computer and at the same time have provided a very popular type of auxiliary storage. In one minute, a typical magnetic tape unit can enter into a computer data that are equivalent to that recorded on 200,000 punched cards. A typical reel of magnetic tape holds 2,400 feet of ½-inch-wide tape and weighs about 4 pounds. The full storage capacity of a reel of tape is approximately equivalent to that contained on 400,000 punched cards. The reader is surely familiar with the large amount of text in the Bible. Seven complete Bibles can be stored on a single reel of magnetic tape, and a tape transport can read or write every word that is in the Bible in less than a minute.

Before the tape unit can perform read or write functions, it must be prepared for operation. This preparation involves loading two reels on the tape

Six magnetic tape transports forming part of an IBM/360 computer system (*Courtesy*, TRW Equipment).

unit (one is empty) and threading the tape through the transport mechanism. The operation is similar to threading a home movie projector.

The magnetic tape unit reads or writes information as the tape moves past the read–write head. Writing on magnetic tape is *destructive;* that is, as new information is written, old information is destroyed. Reading is *nondestructive;* the same information can be read again and again. Information is written on the tape by magnetizing areas in parallel tracks along its length. There are both seven-track and nine-track tapes. There is one write coil in the write head for each recording track. Electrical current flowing through the coils magnetizes the iron oxide coating of the moving tape and erases previously written information.

Computer systems often require a large quantity of storage for data that are to be used only occasionally. In large systems, this requirement is most often met by using magnetic tape. Small computer systems often have the same requirement, although usually on a lesser scale. They cannot use the magnetic tape transports available for large systems because the cost of the transport is generally higher than that of the computer itself. Recently, cassette magnetic tape transports designed as low-cost storage devices for small computers (minicomputers) have been made available.

A *cassette transport* is a digital tape recorder which operates with tape that has been previously loaded in a tape cassette similar to those in a home tape recorder. The cassette, open at one end to permit insertion of magnetic heads and the drive mechanism, contains two reels. The reel hubs are externally driven by the drive mechanism; one end of the tape is fastened to one of the reels, the other end to the second reel. As tape is unwound from one reel, it is transferred to the second.

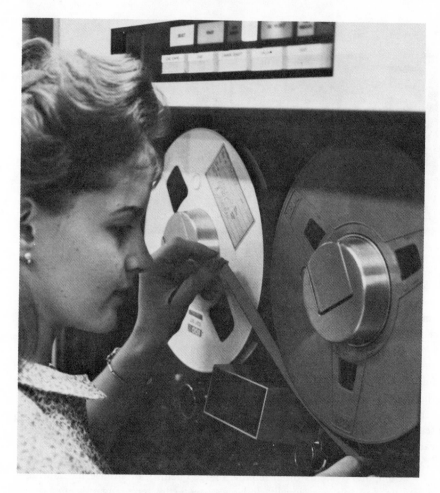

Operator threading magnetic tape through the mechanism of the tape transport (*Courtesy,* American Telephone and Telegraph Co.).

Cassette transports are basically simple, modest-performance devices. Since
they are relatively easy to operate, and their manufacturing cost is fairly low,
they provide a low-cost solution to the problem of large-capacity storage for
small digital computers. Tape cassette units are widely used with microcomputers.

Magnetic Disk Storage

Magnetic disk storage provides computer systems with the ability to
record and retrieve stored data sequentially or randomly. It permits immediate
access to specific areas of information without the need to examine sequentially

A microcomputer system consisting of a microcomputer, keyboard, visual display, and magnetic tape cassette unit (*Courtesy,* PolyMorphic Systems).

all recorded data. Magnetic tape operations do not have this ability; tape searching must start at the beginning of the tape reel and continue sequentially through all records until the desired information area is found.

As an example of the application of *direct access* (sometimes called *random access*) operations as compared to *sequential* operations, consider the act of searching for a word in a large unabridged dictionary. If the contents of the dictionary were stored on magnetic tape, the complete dictionary could be machine-read in approximately two minutes. A wide range of individual words would require an average of one minute for each to be found and read by the sequential method of searching. Using the dictionary, a human being would average approximately one-fifth of a minute per word, simply because he would limit his search for each word to an appropriate portion of the whole dictionary. That is, he would immediately go to a specific letter rather than start at the beginning of the dictionary and check each entry until the right one was found. This concept of limiting a search to a small section of the whole permits direct access storage to perform the dictionary word search in a few thousandths of a second.

The fast speed of access to data storage locations that is provided by magnetic disks permits the user to maintain completely up-to-date data as well as to make rapid reference to previously stored data.

Operator installing a new disk pack on a desk unit (*Courtesy,* U.S. Army Missile Command).

All magnetic disks are physically similar, consisting of thin metal disks coated on both sides with magnetic recording material. The disks are mounted on a vertical shaft at a slight distance from one another to provide space for the

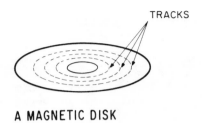

TRACKS

A MAGNETIC DISK

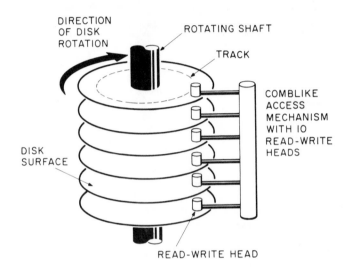

DIRECTION
OF DISK
ROTATION

ROTATING SHAFT

TRACK

COMBLIKE
ACCESS
MECHANISM
WITH 10
READ-WRITE
HEADS

DISK
SURFACE

READ-WRITE HEAD

Magnetic disk access mechanism.

movement of read–write assemblies. The shaft revolves, spinning the disks. Data are stored as magnetized spots in concentric (not spiral) *tracks* on each *surface* of the disk. There are several hundred tracks on each surface. The tracks are accessible for reading and writing by read–write heads that operate between the spinning disks.

Two types of disk units are available. One type uses a stack of permanently fixed disks on which a large amount of data may be stored. The other type uses a removable stack of disks, called a *disk pack*. The removable disk pack unit usually doesn't provide as much direct storage capacity as the larger units made up of many permanently fixed disks. The disk pack is much cheaper, however, and provides almost unlimited storage capacity because it can always be replaced by other packs containing different information. A new pack can be installed on the disk unit in a matter of seconds; in fact, the operation is as simple as loading a reel of magnetic tape on a tape transport.

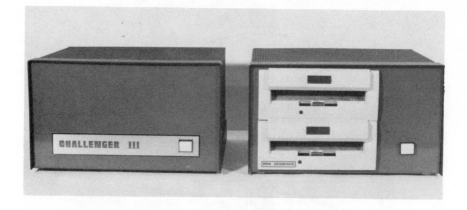

A microcomputer system (left) that includes a floppy disk (right) (*Courtesy, Ohio Scientific*).

disk track: a circular path on a magnetic disk (or drum) for recording data.

disk surface: a flat circular plate coated with some magnetizable material. A large number of **tracks** are available on each surface.

disk pack: a removable disk assembly consisting of a number of disks mounted on a common shaft.

A typical disk assembly has six disks mounted on a vertical shaft and provides ten surfaces on which data can be recorded. The top and bottom surfaces are usually used as protective plates instead of for recording purposes. Information is read from or written on the disk by read—write heads mounted on a comb-like access mechanism consisting of ten heads mounted on five access arms. Each head reads and writes information on its corresponding upper or lower disk surface. The entire access mechanism moves horizontally, making all tracks available for reading and writing.

Disk surfaces can be used repeatedly. Each time new data are stored on a track, the old is erased as the new is recorded. The recorded data may be read as often as desired; data remain recorded in the tracks of a disk until written over.

A new type of disk, recently introduced, has proved to be a strong competitor for the previously mentioned disk units. These disks, called *floppy disks,* are flexible, made of oxide-coated mylar, and stored in paper or plastic envelopes. The entire envelope is inserted in the disk unit effectively protecting the contents of the disk surfaces. The disk surfaces are rotated inside the protective covering. The disk head contacts the track positions through a slot in the covering. Floppy disks are used widely with microcomputers.

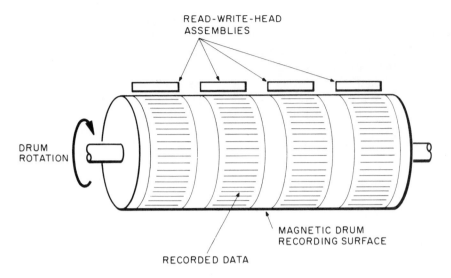

READ-WRITE-HEAD
ASSEMBLIES

DRUM
ROTATION

MAGNETIC DRUM
RECORDING SURFACE

RECORDED DATA

Magnetic drum used as an auxiliary storage device.

Magnetic Drum Storage

In many early computers, the *magnetic drum* was used as the main storage unit. Today, however, it is used exclusively as an auxiliary storage device.

A magnetic drum is a constant-speed, rotating cylinder with an outer surface that is coated with a magnetic material. If an area of this material is placed in a magnetic field, the area will become magnetized. After the magnetic field has been removed, the magnetized spot will remain on the surface of the drum indefinitely. Data so recorded may be read from the drum repeatedly. Recording of new data automatically erases the old. Information is recorded upon, and retrieved from, the rotating drum by read—write heads that are suspended a very slight distance from its periphery. Sending pulses of current to the write coils in the read—write heads magnetizes the drum surface. Conversely, passing the magnetized spots recorded on the drum surface under the read coils allows them to be read. Every drum has a specific number of storage locations, each of which is addressable by the computer. The capacity of each location depends upon the design of the drum and the data code used. Because reading or writing can occur only when a specified location is passing under the heads, access time to data varies in accordance with the distance the addressed location must travel to reach the head.

Magnetic Card and Strip Storage

Both *magnetic card* and *strip* storage provide a means of holding an enormous amount of information at low cost. Magnetic cards and strips are made of the same plastic material as magnetic tape (although considerably thicker) and are coated with the same kind of magnetic material on one side. A number of cards or strips are placed in a cartridge. Like magnetic tapes and disk packs, these cartridges are removable.

The cards (3½ inches by 14 inches) and strips (2¼ inches by 13 inches) are removed from their cartridge whenever data are to be recorded or retrieved. This is done automatically whenever the computer calls for a particular card or strip.

A single card or strip holds thousands of characters of data, and a cartridge stores several million characters.

Laser-Holographic Memory

As computers continue to grow in size and complexity, storage will have to be increased significantly without sacrificing speed. This means the information will have to be packed much more densely in whatever storage device is used. Holography is a technique that can further the development of large storage devices. With recent advances in holography and laser beam technology, computer developers are studying optical memories whose ultimate storage capacity may well be in excess of 100 million bits of data, and whose random access time may be as short as 1 microsecond. Holograms make use of a high-energy laser beam to store or display three-dimensional images. The image produced by a hologram can easily be read by a photodetector, and information can be stored redundantly.

A holographic memory is made on a special recording medium somewhat similar to conventional photographic film. The recording process starts with the construction of a data mask that represents the contents of a page. Each mask is basically an array of pinholes, blocked where zeros are to be recorded and transparent where ones are needed. Each data mask is recorded holographically, one at a time, on the recording medium. Information is retrieved from the memory by projecting the data recorded on the hologram onto a light-sensitive detector. The detector converts the optical information into electronic signals that the computer can process.

Thin Film

Thin film storage, which utilizes concepts similar to those magnetic core storage is based on, has been used as internal storage for some recently developed computers. It is, however, more compact, more expensive, and faster in access time than magnetic core storage.

One form of thin film memory consists of a series of metallic alloy dots, a few millionths of an inch thick, deposited on a glass, ceramic, or plastic plate. The metallic dots are connected by very fine wires and perform in the same manner as magnetic cores. Like magnetic cores, these dots can be magnetized in either of two stable preferred directions. Several thousand dots may be deposited on a glass, ceramic, or plastic plate. The metallic dots are connected by very fine wires and perform in the same manner as magnetic cores. Like magnetic cores, these dots can be magnetized in either of two stable preferred directions. Several thousand dots may be deposited on a 1-inch square plane.

Because the thin film consist of so many small spots, the arrangement of circuits to perform reading and writing operations is difficult. A common method is to etch copper wires onto an insulating material. Then, by closely positioning these circuits, the spots can be magnetized and their direction of magnetization sensed.

Virtual Memory

System designers and programmers have typically had to be concerned with internal memory capacity to make sure that they could fit their computer programs and working data into the available space. If the programs were too large for memory, the programmer would segment the program, putting the first part in internal storage and the other segments in auxiliary or secondary storage. When the first section was complete, the second section would be brought into internal storage (overlaid in the same memory area that contained the first section). The use of overlays can be limited to smaller sections, so that a main segment is kept intact and smaller portions are overlaid.

The concept of *virtual memory* is to have the hardware and software *automatically* segment the program and to move segments into storage when needed. The auxiliary storage, usually disk units, is in effect utilized as an "extension" of the computer's internal memory. Virtual memory is the memory space defined by a range of addresses specified by the programmer and different from the addresses utilized by the memory system. A device is required for translating the addresses used by the program into the correct memory location addresses. The size of virtual memory is consequently limited only by the addressing capability of the computer and not by the number of locations in its internal memory. With virtual memory, the programmer has the illusion that the memory of the computer is larger than it really is.

The basic element of a virtual memory is a program segment or page—a fixed-size unit of storage, usually 2,048 or 4,096 bytes. The pages of memory are swapped back and forth in such a way that the internal memory (real memory) of the computer is expanded to many times its actual capacity. The process of swapping programs or data back and forth is referred to as *page-in*, since the page goes from disk to internal memory, and *page-out* as a page leaves the internal memory and is stored on the disk unit.

The difficult part of any memory organization is keeping track of what part of the program is in internal storage and what part is stored on the disk. A technique called *dynamic memory allocation* is used in the management of memory resources. This technique divides a selected area of internal memory into pages. Any available page may be assigned for different purposes, depending on the requirements of the moment. A control routine keeps account of which pages are free so that the available memory space can be immediately assigned as needed. This is accomplished by a technique wherein available pages are linked together in the form of a chain. When a memory page becomes available, it is appropriately added to the chain. The control routine shuffles programs or data from auxiliary storage into available memory pages as required.

An IBM virtual memory system has a special hardware device, called a *dynamic address translation (DAT)* device, which is used to control the memory allocation assignments. Other computer manufacturers use software techniques (part of the operating system) to control dynamic memory allocation assignments.

Virtual memory allows a programmer to write a program as if internal memory were limitless. With virtual memory, the computer takes care of the difficulty of scheduling the swapping of data and programs.

Questions

1. Distinguish between main and auxiliary storage.
2. Main storage is not directly accessible by the central processor. True or false?
3. In what way does direct access processing differ from sequential access processing?
4. What is a magnetic core?
5. Under what condition is a core said to be "on or 1"? "Off or 0"?
6. What is a memory plane? Where are magnetic cores located on a memory plane?
7. What is the most common main memory of computers?
8. What is meant by *access time? Capacity?*
9. Explain the following terms: (a) *record*, (b) *file*, and (c) *unit*.
10. What are some advantages of direct-access storage devices?
11. Define the following terms: (a) *address*, (b) *word*, (c) *byte*.
12. Magnetic tape is frequently used for recording and storing data because it feeds data slowly into the computer. True or false?
13. Magnetic disks are called direct-access devices because data is stored at a unique location on a disk where it can be retrieved at will by the computer. True or false?
14. Magnetic cards are simply ordinary punched cards in which the holes are magnetized. True or false?
15. Can a magnetic tape system be called a direct-access device? If not, why not?

16. What is a semiconductor memory?
17. Why do microcomputer manufacturers use semiconductor memory as the main memory?
18. Why does the virtual memory concept permit the user to run larger programs than could be run without virtual memory?
19. What is a page?
20. What is meant by "page-in"? "Page-out"?

6

Designing the Computer Program

Introduction

Without a program, a computer is a helpless collection of electronic circuitry. With a proper program, a computer can direct city traffic, play chess, navigate ships, compose music, or guide a satellite into orbit. In this chapter, we will examine some of the techniques which are used to develop computer programs.

program: a series of instructions that determines the operation of a computer.

A computer does not do any thinking and cannot make unplanned decisions. Every step of each problem it handles has to be accounted for by a program. If, for example, you were requested to eat your dinner in computer language, the program might involve the following steps:

1. Extend hand to fork
2. Pick up fork
3. Decide what to eat: peas, meat, or potatoes
   a. Don't like meat so push it to other side of plate
   b. Potatoes are not cooked properly so don't eat them
   c. Are peas hot?
   d. If they are, wait until they cool
   e. If they aren't, proceed to eat peas
4. Straighten arm so fork touches peas
5. Scoop a few peas onto fork
6. Bend arm up so peas reach mouth
7. Open mouth
8. Insert peas
9. Remove fork

10. Close mouth
11. Return fork to table
12. Chew peas
13. Swallow peas
14. Are there still peas on the plate?
    a. If there are, go back to step 3
    b. If not, burp and get up from the table

A problem need not be described by an exact mathematical equation to be solvable by a computer, but it does need a definite set of rules that the computer can follow. If a problem requires intuition or guessing, or is so hard to define that it cannot be put into precise words, the computer cannot solve it. A great deal of thought must be put into defining the problem exactly and setting it up for the computer in such a way that every possible alternative is taken care of.

When you begin to develop a program, you must be familiar with several aspects of the situation:

1. You must thoroughly understand the problem and be able to determine if it is feasible to solve it on a computer.
2. You must know what operations can be performed by the computer available.
3. You must understand what the program output is to be.

You should remember that computers are used to implement solutions to problems. Computers do not solve problems; *people* solve problems. The computer carries out the solution as specified by people.

There are five steps involved in the solution of a problem with a computer:

1. Problem analysis
2. Flowcharting
3. Writing the program
4. Testing the program
5. Documentation.

We will now consider each of these steps.

Problem Analysis

Before a problem can be solved on a computer, the following questions must be answered:

- Is the problem worth doing?
- Can the problem be solved with a computer?
- How can the problem be solved on a computer?
- Can the computer in question solve the problem?
- What are the inputs and outputs?

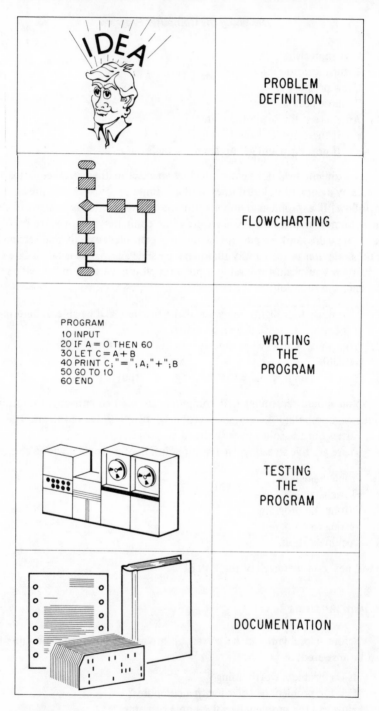

	PROBLEM DEFINITION
	FLOWCHARTING
PROGRAM 10 INPUT 20 IF A = 0 THEN 60 30 LET C = A + B 40 PRINT C; " = "; A; " + "; B 50 GO TO 10 60 END	WRITING THE PROGRAM
	TESTING THE PROGRAM
	DOCUMENTATION

Prescribed pattern for the solving of any problem on a computer involves the five steps shown.

- What programming language will be used?
- Have parts of the problem already been programmed?

The principal job of problem analysis is to define the problem properly. Although it may sound strange to say so, we must know exactly what the problem is before we attempt to solve it.

People often ask such questions as, "Can you play chess with a computer?" "Can you simulate the operations of a jet aircraft with a computer?" "Can you automate a business accounting system on a computer?" "Can you monitor the operation of a plant with a computer?" Of course, all of these things can be accomplished with a computer, but it may first take several months or even years to define the problem adequately. Generally, a problem can be considered defined when all inputs and outputs have been identified, when the outputs have been determined to be correct, and a solution to the problem can be flowcharted.

Once the problem has been defined, it is then necessary to select a method of solution which will identify the sequence of logical and arithmetic operations needed to solve the problem.

Flowcharting

After we analyze a problem, we must make a *flowchart* of the solution. A flowchart is a drawing which helps to define the problem or, in other words, a pictorial view of the logic used to solve the problem. It is composed of a sequence of special symbols connected by straight lines.

flowchart: a pictorial diagram of a sequence of steps required to solve a problem, usually drawn with conventional symbols representing different types of events and their interconnections.

There are several reasons for drawing flowcharts:

- To present the logic used in solving a problem in pictorial form.
- To provide a way of communicating the program logic to other people.
- To divide a large problem into several smaller manageable segments. The smaller segments can be coded without regard to the complete problem. Flowcharts show the relationship of one part of a program to another.
- To provide a visual description of the data process, which allows better control over computer operations.
- To provide a detailed blueprint to be used in writing the computer program.

Flowcharts are perhaps the best method available for expressing what computers can do, or what you want them to do. They are simple, easy to prepare and use, and eliminate ambiguities.

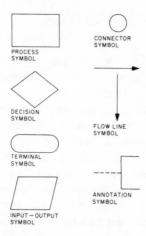

Commonly used flowcharting symbols.

Flowcharts have various levels of detail. Some are very general whereas others include completely detailed steps. The flowchart drawn in the first stages of program design usually shows fewer steps than those developed further along in the planning. Many programmers go through several stages of flowcharting before actually writing the program instructions. Others write instructions at once. It is a matter of personal preference and experience. At each stage, however, the level of detail must be sufficient for unambiguous coding of the program.

flowcharting symbols: conventional diagrammatic representations of different events which are shown on a flowchart.

The most commonly used *flowcharting symbols,* which may vary in size, are as follows:

- The *process symbol,* which is used to define a process, a set of operations, a single operation, or an arithmetic calculation. Always used for any operation not specified by one of the symbols below.
- The *decision symbol,* which is used whenever a decision, a logical choice, or a conditional branch is to be made. The results of the decision will determine the next step to be taken in the program.
- The *terminal symbol,* which is used to indicate the start of a program or the end of a program.
- The *input-output symbol,* which is used to indicate an input or output operation not specified by a special symbol.
- The *connector symbol,* which is used to connect the logic flow of a

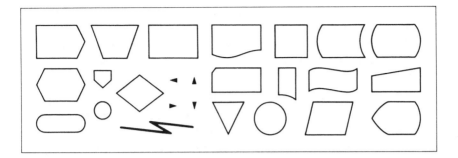

Template used to simplify drawing of flowcharts (*Courtesy,* IBM Corp.).

Programmer preparing a flowchart with the aid of a programming template
(*Courtesy,* IBM Corp.).

flowchart (most often for unconditional branches). A connector pair
includes one numbered circle which marks the end of a flowline. The same
number in another connector symbol shows the connection of that flowline.

- The *flowline symbol,* which is used to show the continuity of operations. Direction is indicated by arrows.
- The *annotation symbol,* which is used to add descriptive comments or explanatory notes for human communication only.

Whenever possible, it is preferred that flowcharts be drawn using flow directions of top-to-bottom and left-to-right. They may be drawn on paper of any size, although standard 8½ x 11″ paper is sometimes preferred. Rough flowcharts can be prepared by sketching the symbols on paper, but a much better flowchart can be made by using a *template,* a clear plastic plate that contains cutouts of the flowcharting symbols.

template: a plastic guide containing cutouts of the conventional flowcharting symbols and used as an aid in drawing flowcharts.

The following pages show sample flowcharts. One defines the logic of a candy machine that delivers a 15-cent candy bar plus change for any input of nickels, dimes, and quarters. Other coins are rejected. The second is the flowchart for an altitude conversion program. It converts altitude figures expressed in feet (the ordinary unit for aircraft) into figures expressed in miles (one mile equals 5,280 feet) and then prints a table giving both values for a range of 0 to 200,000 feet in steps of 10,000 feet.

Coding the Program

Coding is the name given to the writing of instructions for a sequence of computer operations. Normally, one codes from flowcharts. A single flowchart symbol may result in several computer instructions. These are recorded on preprinted coding sheets and then usually keypunched onto punched cards.

The flowchart for the altitude conversion problem just discussed might be coded as follows:

```
10  REM ALTITUDE CONVERSION PROGRAM
20  PRINT "ALT IN FEET," "ALT IN MILES"
30  FOR F = 0 TO 200000 STEP 10000
40      REM COMPUTE ALTITUDE IN MILES
50      LET M = F/5280
60      PRINT F, M
70  NEXT F
80  END
```

This program would print the following table (partial):

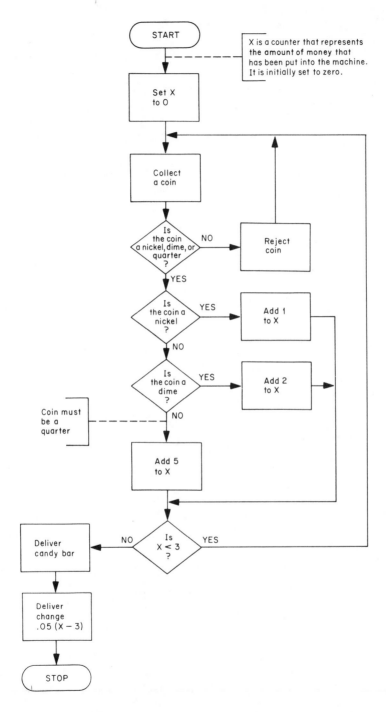

Flowchart of the logic of a candy machine that delivers a 15-cent candy bar plus change for any input of nickels, dimes, and quarters.

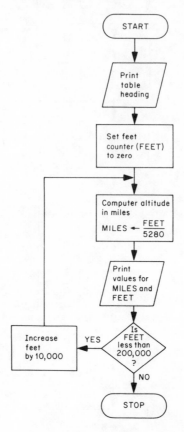

Flowchart for an altitude conversion program.

ALT IN FEET	ALT IN MILES
0	0
10000	1.89394
20000	3.78788
30000	5.68182
40000	7.57576
50000	9.46970
60000	11.36360
⋮	⋮

Few people can write a program involving a hundred or more statements without error. What type of errors do they make? A few are listed below:

- Keypunching errors
- Confusion of characters, for example, S for 5, 1 for I, Z for 2.

- Undefined symbols
- Ambiguous decisions
- Unprogrammed branches

Many program mistakes can be found by reviewing the flowcharts of processing operations and associated coding sheets very carefully, sometimes by individuals other than the one who drew up the program. This checking process is often called *desk checking* or *desk debugging*. Desk checks may not detect all errors (often called *bugs*), but they detect enough to make them worthwhile.

coding: the writing of instructions for a computer.

After all mistakes detected in the desk check have been diagnosed and corrected, the program is ready to be translated into instructions that the computer understands. The translation process will be discussed in detail in the next chapter.

Debugging the Program

After the program has been translated into a language that the computer understands, it is necessary to execute the program on the computer to determine if it works properly (it usually does not on the first try) and, if not, to make the required program revisions to make it do so. This step is called program testing or *debugging*.

Programming is an exercise in logical thinking. There is no place for loose ends or fuzzy reasoning. Otherwise, program mistakes are bound to occur that will show up during the testing process.

debugging: the process of testing a program for the purpose of detecting and correcting errors.

bug: an informal term used to indicate mistakes in a program caused by human error.

It is a good idea to remember some of the so-called axioms of programming:

- Every computer program contains at least one bug.
- If there is a bug, the computer will find it.
- If anything can go wrong, it will.

Documentation

After the program is working, a programmer should put together a documentation package for others to use. This package should include at least the following items:

Programmers attempting to find an error in a program (*Courtesy,* IBM Corp.).

- An English language description of the problem
- A flowchart
- A printout of the program instructions
- A list of instructions needed to operate the program
- Sample program output
- A list of error conditions
- A deck of punched cards or roll of punched paper tape containing the program.

Documentation of programs contributes to their useful value. Well documented programs are extremely valuable, for example, whenever the program is to be rewritten on another computer or whenever someone other than the originator has to modify the program.

Structured Programming

Structured programming is concerned with improving the programming process through better organization of programs and better programming notation to facilitate correct and clear descriptions of data and control structures.

Improved programming languages and organized programming techniques should help one produce programs that are: (1) more understandable and therefore more easily modified and documented, (2) more economical to run because good organization and notation make it easier for a compiler to "understand" the program's logic, and (3) more correct and therefore more easily debugged.

The physical structure of a well-organized program corresponds to the sequence of steps in the algorithm being implemented. At a lower level all parts of the implementation of one idea are grouped in a structure that clearly indicates how the various parts are selected and sequenced and the relation of this idea to neighboring ideas.

The program should be expressed in the most natural and appropriate representation. The program should not contain a GOTO statement when a better representation is available. A program designer should, however, use a GOTO statement when the alternates are worse. Whenever a GOTO statement is used in a program, it should be accompanied by enough comment to make its purpose perfectly clear.

Some program designers limit their conception of structured programs to programs with structured control and ignore the equally important factor of structured data. When the data have to be manipulated to fit the available data structure representations, the program becomes less readable. The program designer should inform the reader and the computer how to represent his data structure representations into the computer's representations, and then go about using his representations in his program.

A good language for structured programming has a carefully thought out assortment of control structures and data structure definition facilities. If a language provides one kind of iterative control statement for counter-controlled loops and others for loops controlled by a decision value of an expression, then the former should be used when the loop is expected to terminate as a result of the counter's reaching its terminal value, and the others should be used when some other condition is expected to terminate the loop. This makes it easier for a reader to distinguish the "nature" of the control being exercised by the loop.

When a line of code is a continuation of a previous line or a subsidiary idea, it should be indented from the left margin established by the principal statement. When an indented code might be so complex or long as to obscure the principal level of control, then one should consider making this code into a procedure. A good rule of thumb is to try to get each principal idea to fit on a single page.

Structured programming is often associated with "top-down programming." Although this technique is a useful tool for explaining a program and illustrates how much nicer it is to explain a structured program than a haphazardly written one, it is unlikely that the art of programming can be restricted to the use of a single technique.

Questions

1. Discuss the main aspects of the problem situation with which you must be concerned before developing a program.
2. List the five steps that are used in the solution of a problem by a computer.
3. Explain the reasons for using each of the five steps mentioned above.
4. Any problem can be solved on a computer. True or false?
5. What is a flowchart? Name several reasons for using one.
6. Draw a flowchart to show the sequence of events in getting up any morning of the week and in carrying out your subsequent morning activities after you get up.
7. Draw a flowchart that will analyze a poker hand.
8. Draw a flowchart to play the game of tic-tac-toe.
9. Define *coding*.
10. Why is it necessary to test or debug a program?
11. What is meant by structured programming?

7

The Language of the Computer

What Is Programming?

The key to the successful use of a computer is *programming*. The computer cannot even add two numbers unless it has been so directed. In fact, the simplest task can be a major problem for the computer if it has been poorly programmed, and paradoxically, a complex problem can be a simple task when properly programmed.

> **programming:** the process by which a set of instructions is produced for a computer to make it perform some specified activity. The activity can be anything from the solution of a complex engineering problem to the reservation of airline seats.

Programming involves writing in sequence a set of instructions that will produce a desired result when the sequence is executed on the computer. These instructions are stored in the memory of the computer. The data upon which these operations are performed are also stored in the computer's memory.

Writing a computer program in English simplifies the writing process because the program is stated in terms that we understand. However, a program so written has no meaning to a computer since it does not "understand" the English language. Therefore, the program must be written in the language of the computer if it is to be understood by the computer.

As stated in Chapter 6, the writing of computer instructions is called *coding*. Coding a program for a computer can take place at three levels of computer languages: *machine language* (the basic language of the computer), *assembler language* (a low-level symbolic language), and *compiler language* (a high-level symbolic language).

Since both assembler and compiler languages are symbolic in nature, they must be converted into machine language instructions prior to their *execution* on a computer. Since the computer operates strictly at the level of machine coding, all other codes must eventually be converted into that form.

execution: performance of the operations specified by the instructions of a program.

The Stored Program Concept

The first electronic digital computer, ENIAC, was directed to perform its functions by means of wired control panels and switches. ENIAC had more than a hundred control lines along which instructions could be sent. Basically, ENIAC could be instructed to solve a problem in two ways: the plugging of the control lines into sockets or hubs and the setting of switches. The difficulty with ENIAC was that, with each new problem, a new set of control lines had to be plugged into different sockets to enter the new set of instructions. Sometimes it took several days to perform this operation.

Even before ENIAC was completed, a group at the Moore School of Electrical Engineering of the University of Pennsylvania talked over ideas for a new machine, EDVAC, which was to have an internally stored program. As a result of these talks, John von Neumann wrote a document in 1945 entitled *First Draft of a Report on the EDVAC.* Imbedded in this document was the remarkable idea of the stored program. He suggested that the instructions for the computer—previously entered on punched paper tape or by wired plugboards—could be stored in the computer's electronic memory as numbers and treated in exactly the same manner as numerical data.

For the first time, then, logical choices of program sequences could be made *inside* the machine, and the instructions could be modified by the computer as it went along. Another stored-program computer, called the EDSAC, was being developed at Cambridge University in England at about the same time. This computer used the same concepts that von Neumann had proposed for the EDVAC. Today, all computers use the stored-program concept.

Machine Language Programming

Inside the computer, all instructions are executed by means of electronic pulses, and the language used is binary. A *machine language* instruction consists of a string of bits that directs the computer to perform some specific operation, such as add, subtract, multiply, divide, store, load, read, write, shift, and so on. The string of bits, 100011, could, for example, be used to indicate a multiply operation.

A machine language instruction consists of an *operation code* and one or more *operands.* The operation code specifies the operation that is to be performed. The operands identify the quantities to be operated on, for example, the numbers to be added or the locations where data are stored.

machine language program: the set of instructions written in machine code which can immediately be obeyed by a computer without translation.

operation code: the code which specifies the particular **operation** to be performed.

operation: an action defined by part of a single computer instruction.

operand: a quantity in an instruction—for example, a result, an argument, or a number—the address portion of an instruction, or an indication of the location of the next instruction.

Consider the following machine language instruction with two operands.

Operation Code	Operand 1	Operand 2
011100	000011	010110100011000

The operation code refers to the part of the instruction that specifies the operation to be performed, such as *add* or *read.* The operands refer to the part of the instruction that references the location within the computer where the data to be processed can be found. In the example, the operation code 011100 indicates that the computer is to perform an addition operation. The operand 010110100011000 specifies the computer storage location of the data to be added to the data located in register 000011 (specified by operand 1).

It should be obvious to the reader that working with machine language instructions (a string of 1's and 0's) is a tedious and cumbersome task. This is why machine language programming is rarely (if ever) used today.

Machine language coding can be simplified somewhat by representing the *binary* machine language instruction as an instruction in some other number base, say *octal.* The previous instruction would then look like the following.

Operation Code	Operand 1	Operand 2
34	03	26430

Although the octal instruction is somewhat simpler, it is also rather clumsy to use since it has no easily recognizable symbolic aspects.

binary system: a number system using the base two. The two binary digits are zero and one.

octal system: a number system using the base eight. The octal system uses the digits 0, 1, 2, 3, 4, 5, 6, and 7. Octal notation may be used as a shorthand way of representing a string of bits. For example, the binary number 001000111 can be considered as being formed by the three binary coded octal numbers 001 000 111, that is, 107. Thus the binary number 001000111 can be represented as octal 107.

A short machine language program is shown below. Octal notation is used to represent the instructions.

Machine Language Coding Form

Storage location of instruction	Operation code	Operand 1	Operand 2	Comments
3001	42	07	26400	Load register with c
3002	14	07	32000	Multiply by b
3003	34	07	25300	Add a
3004	27	07	41000	Store as d

The previous program computes a value for d in accordance with the equation

$$d = a + (b \times c)$$

Although machine languages provide economy of construction, they are usually inconvenient for direct human use since they require that the user have a thorough knowledge of the computer, its peculiarities and intricate details. It was inevitable that numbers should be replaced by symbols and words that could be better understood by the user.

Symbolic Languages

Symbolic languages were developed to overcome some of the many inconveniences of machine languages. A computer can be programmed to recognize instructions in one of these languages and then to convert these instructions into machine language, thus freeing the user of having to do so himself.

symbolic language: a programming language, also called **source language,** in which operation codes and data items (operands) may be assigned symbolic designations.

Before looking at symbolic languages more closely, let us define several terms. As stated earlier, a *program* is a meaningful sequence of instructions or statements. *Statements,* in turn, are strings of symbols from a given *alphabet,* composed of letters, digits, and special characters. The form of each statement obeys a set of rules (*syntax*) and possesses an operational meaning (*semantics*). Collectively, the alphabet, syntax, and semantics are termed a *language.* A *source program* is a computer program written in a symbolic language. The instructions or statements of a source program are processed in the computer in order to produce a program that can eventually be executed on the machine. This processing function is called *translating,* and the processor program is called a *translator.* Thus, the translator converts a program written in symbolic language into machine language. This machine language program is called an *object program.* A translator thus converts a source program into an object program. The object program is the program that is executed on the computer to produce the desired results.

statement: a source language instruction.

syntax: the rules which govern the structure of language statements; in particular, the rules for forming statements in a source language correctly (such as those for punctuations, etc., in English).

semantics: the meaning of a language

source program: a program written in a symbolic language, for later conversion to an object program.

object program: a machine language program that is executed by a computer.

translator: a computer program which converts statements written in one programming language to the format of another programming language, for example, from a source language to an object language.

Symbolic languages are more suitable for human use than machine languages, greatly facilitate computer programming, and tend to be more directly associated in some sense with the actual problems under consideration. One of the features that speeded their widespread acceptance is the fact that computer programs written in them may be readily translated to machine language by another computer program running on the same or even a different type of computer. One of the significant aspects of the philosophy behind the use of symbolic languages and translating programs is the fact that the same type of computer may process programs written in many different languages, provided only that a separate translator program has been written for each language.

Assembler Language Programming

The symbolic language that most closely resembles machine language is called *assembler language*. It is sometimes called a *low-level programming language* or a *machine-oriented language*. In this language, all operation codes of the computer are given a mnemonic designation. All machine addresses and other operands in the instructions are written using symbolic notation. This type of language relieves the programmer of many intricate coding details; however, it takes as many symbolic instructions to solve a problem as it does machine instructions. As in machine-language coding, the user must have a thorough knowledge of the computer and its operation.

> **assembler language:** a low-level symbolic programming language. Assembly language instructions are written on the basis of a subsequent one-for-one conversion from machine-language instructions.

There are three major advantages to using assembler language code rather than machine code:

- It is easier to write.
- It is easier to read.
- It is easier to modify.

A statement in assembler language consists of from one to four entries—location, operation, operand, comment. An add operation (with no location specified) in assembler language would look like the following:

ADD REG3, TEMP

The ADD in the above instructions is the symbolic code for the addition operation, and REG3 and TEMP in the operand portion of the instruction provide a symbolic representation of the two storage locations. If we wanted to compute $d = a + (b \times c)$ in assembler language, we might write the sequence of symbolic instructions shown in the coding form.

Assembler Language Coding Form

Location	Operation	Operand 1	Operand 2	Comments
BEGIN	LDA	REG3	C	Load C into register 3
	MUL	REG3	B	Multiply register 3 by B
	ADD	REG3	A	Add A to register 3
	STR	REG3	D	Store register 3 at D

Before the computer can use this program, it is necessary for it to translate these symbolic instructions into machine language form. The translator used to convert assembler language programs to object programs is called an *assembler.*

> **assembler:** a computer program that accepts source statements written in an assembler language and converts them into machine language instructions for the computer in which the program is to be used.

The procedure used for assembling an assembler language program is as follows. Prior to assembling the program, the assembler must be placed in the computer's main storage. Then the source program, written in assembly language, is presented to the computer. The assembler then converts each symbolic statement into a machine usable form. The computer does not execute the converted statements but instead records the object program on punched cards, punched paper tape, magnetic tape, magnetic disk, or whatever. Now the object program is placed into the computer again, and this time the computer will execute the machine language instructions and produce the calculated results. Note that the program had to be presented to the computer twice, the first time in assembler language (the human being's language) and the second time in object language (the machine's language).

Although assembler languages were certainly a significant improvement over machine languages, they were still machine dependent, that is, every type of computer has its own assembler language.

Compiler Language Programming

In contrast to assembler languages and machine languages in which the source language is still highly dependent upon a particular computer, *compiler languages* relate much more closely to the procedures being coded and are thus relatively machine independent. A program coded in a compiler language can thus be executed on any computer system which has a translator available for that language. Compiler language is sometimes called *high-level language, procedure-oriented language,* or *problem-oriented language.*

> **compiler language:** a high-level symbolic programming language, a single statement of which may cause several machine language instructions to be generated.

In the mid 1950s, Dr. Grace Murray Hopper, then a Senior Mathematician at the Eckert-Mauchly Computer Corp. (the forerunner of the present Univac Division of Sperry Rand Corporation) developed a concept of *automatic programming* with a compiling system which enabled the computer to write its own program from a small subset of English language instructions. From this original

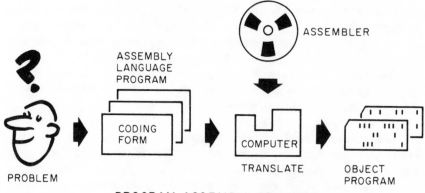

PROGRAM ASSEMBLY PROCESS

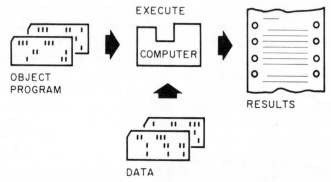

EXECUTE PROGRAM PROCESS

An assembler is used to convert assembler language programs into computer-usable form, such as the punched cards shown here.

concept, she developed the first English language compiler system, FLOMATIC, later incorporated into the very widely used compiler language, COBOL.

automatic programming: a method by which a computer converts program statements written in symbolic form into the machine language of the computer.

About the same time, a group of IBM personnel headed by John Backus was developing a programming system which was later to become the most widely used compiler language in the world. This language was called FORTRAN and was first developed for the IBM 704 computer.

Compiler languages are essentially general in application, although among the contemporary systems several are clearly better adapted to problems of a numerical type and others to nonnumerical applications. Three of the more popular numerically oriented compiler languages are FORTRAN, BASIC, and APL, whereas popular compiler languages for nonnumerical applications are COBOL and RPG. A compiler language designed for multipurpose use (both numerical and nonnumerical problems) is called PL/I.

Many compiler languages have been introduced in recent years, primarily because this type of language simplifies the programming task. The user is no longer required to have a detailed knowledge of computers and is thus able to concentrate more thoroughly on steps more closely related to the problem. Compiler languages are widely accepted and can be used by persons not having a strong background in machine language programming or computer equipment.

A program can be written in a much shorter time period when a compiler language is used, primarily because the language includes a set of very powerful statements. A single compiler language statement can accomplish an operation that would require several dozen lower-level machine instructions. Both coding and debugging tasks are also simplified.

The computer is rather good at the translation process, thus allowing us to write programs in a language that is convenient to us and to place on the computer the whole burden of translating them into a set of instructions which it can then execute. There is no need to address the computer in *its* language; we can instruct it to act upon commands from *our* language.

The translator for compiler languages is called a *compiler*. How do we teach the computer to accept a compiler language? Well, since the computer can do only what we order it to do, a compiler must be placed in its memory before the source language program is read in.

compiler: a computer program that accepts source statements written in compiler language and converts them into machine language instructions for the computer in which the program is to be used.

For input, the compiler uses the source language program. The object program is the compiler's output. The compiler is like a foreman, who interprets and amplifies the manager's instructions for a workman. The compiler is prepared only once and must be stored in the computer before any source program is read in.

As in the assembling process, the procedure of carrying out a particular computation consists of two stages. First the source language program is translated, or compiled, into the equivalent object program; and second, the object program is executed. The two stages are kept separate. Compilation is completed before any actual computation begins, and in fact the entire object program is stored before any part of it is executed.

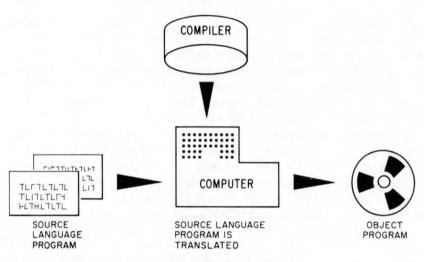

COMPILE PROGRAM PROCESS

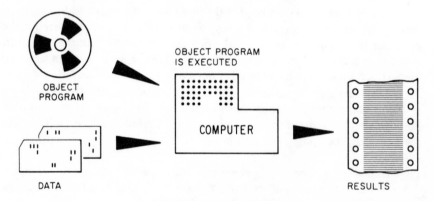

EXECUTE PROGRAM PROCESS

A compiler is used to translate source language programs written in a compiler language into a computer-usable form, such as the magnetic tape shown here.

At the completion of the compilation, one of two things may happen. The object program may be immediately executed, or it may be recorded, for later use, on some suitable medium, such as punched cards, punched paper tape, magnetic tape, or magnetic disk. In the latter case, the object program must be read back into the computer before it can be executed. The two-stage process allows the source language program to be compiled on one computer and later

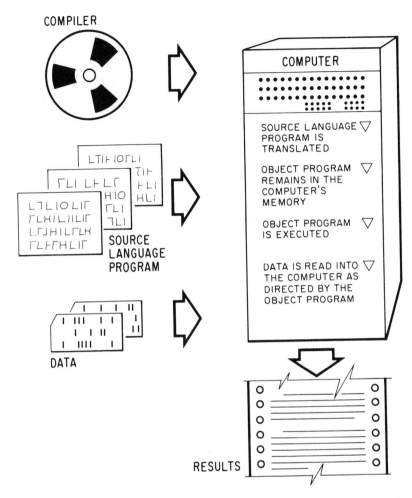

COMPILER

COMPUTER

SOURCE LANGUAGE ▽
PROGRAM IS
TRANSLATED

OBJECT PROGRAM ▽
REMAINS IN THE
COMPUTER'S
MEMORY

OBJECT PROGRAM ▽
IS EXECUTED

DATA IS READ INTO ▽
THE COMPUTER AS
DIRECTED BY THE
OBJECT PROGRAM

SOURCE
LANGUAGE
PROGRAM

DATA

RESULTS

Steps of the compile-and-go process used in translating the source program and immediately executing the generated object program.

executed on the same or a different computer. The compile-and-immediately-execute process is often called the *compile-and-go* process.

compile-and-go: an automatic procedure that compiles the source language program and immediately executes the object program.

Both assemblers and compilers offer auxiliary functions that assist the user in documenting and correcting the statements written. These functions include program listings and error indications when errors are detected during the translating process.

Special programs such as compilers and assemblers are referred to generically as *software*, as opposed to *hardware*, which refers to actual computer equipment.

software: the programs which can be used on a computer.

hardware: the physical units making up a computer system.

The FORTRAN Language

FORTRAN, an acronym derived from *FORmula TRANslation*, is a scientifically oriented programming language first developed in 1957. It has a great deal of machine independence and is probably the most widely used compiler language in the world, partly because FORTRAN compilers have been developed for most computers now in use. The language was designed primarily for solving scientific and engineering problems, although some commercial business installations use it as well.

Because of FORTRAN's close similarity to mathematical notation, it is easy to learn and use. For example, mathematical expressions such as $y = ax + bz + 36$ can be written in the FORTRAN language as

$$Y = A * X + B * Z + 36$$

A brief **FORTRAN** program will now be discussed. Let us consider the writing of a **FORTRAN** program to convert Fahrenheit temperature readings to equivalent readings in Celsius (centigrade), Kelvin, and Rankine.

Fahrenheit temperature values may be converted to Celsius values by subtracting 32° from the Fahrenheit temperature reading and then multiplying the difference by 5/9 (reference equation 1).

$$°C = 5/9 \, (°F - 32°) \tag{1}$$

Kelvin temperature may be obtained by adding 273° to a Celsius value (reference equation 2):

$$°K = °C + 273° \tag{2}$$

A Rankine measurement can be obtained by adding 460° to a Fahrenheit value (reference equation 3).

$$°R = °F + 460° \tag{3}$$

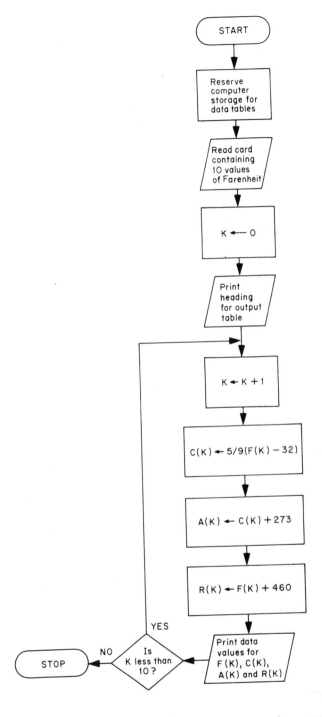

Flowchart used to prepare the FORTRAN temperature conversion program.

The following FORTRAN program, coded from the flowchart shown, will convert ten Fahrenheit values to their equivalent values in Celsius, Kelvin, and Rankine:

```
C       TEMPERATURE CONVERSION PROGRAM
        DIMENSION F(10), C(10), A(10), R(10)
C       READ CARD CONTAINING 10 FAHRENHEIT VALUES
        READ (5, 10) F
    10  FORMAT (10F5.0)
        K = 0
C       PRINT HEADING
        WRITE (6,20)
    20  FORMAT (34H1 FAHRENHEIT CELSIUS KELVIN RANKINE)
        K = 0
    30  K = K + 1
        C(K) = 5.0/9.0 * (F(K) - 32.0)
        A(K) = C(K) + 273.0
        R(K) = F(K) + 460.0
C       PRINT VALUES FOR F,C,A and R
        WRITE (6,40) F(K), C(K), A(K), R(K)
    40  FORMAT (1H0F3.0, 4X, F8.4, 4X, F7.3, 4X, F4.0)
        IF (K .LT. 10) GO TO 30
        STOP
        END
```

This FORTRAN program reads a data card that contains the ten values of Fahrenheit temperatures. The program then performs the conversions for all values and causes the equivalent of the following table of values to be printed:

FAHRENHEIT	CELSIUS	KELVIN	RANKINE
144.	62.2222	335.222	604.
36.	2.2222	275.222	496.
110.	43.3333	316.333	570.
98.	36.6667	309.667	558.
63.	17.2222	290.222	523.
26.	−3.3333	269.667	486.
14.	−10.0000	263.000	474.
78.	25.5556	298.556	538.
66.	18.8889	291.889	526.
51.	10.5556	283.556	511.

The COBOL Language

COBOL is an acronym for *COmmon Business-Oriented Language*. The COBOL language provides a link between business English and the language of the computer. It is based on the use of English words (about 250 of them) and certain rules of syntax derived from English. However, since it is a language to be processed by a computer, it must be a very precise language.

The COBOL language uses nouns, verbs, connectives, and sentences. Many of the statements are self-explanatory even to those who have never used a computer, for example:

>READ INPUT-FILE AND GO TO EOT
>IF TOTAL-PAY IS LESS THAN
>ADD OVERTIME-PAY TO TOTAL-PAY
>ADD WKPAY TO REGISTER
>CLOSE INPUT-FILE
>END-OF-RUN
>OUTPUT CUSTOMER-BILL-FILE

A COBOL program is divided into four parts, called *divisions.* The Procedure Division describes the internal processing that the computer is to perform. The Identification Division is used to attach identifications such as program name, program number, programmer's name, and the like to the program. The Environment Division is used to specify the computer on which the program is to be compiled and executed. The Data Division is used to define the characteristics and format of the data to be processed.

The sample program shown below illustrates the COBOL language. Normally the program is prepared on a COBOL PROGRAM SHEET and then transferred to 80-column punched cards. This sample program calculates the product of the values 643 and 746 and causes the product to be printed on the line printer.

>IDENTIFICATION DIVISION.
>PROGRAM-ID. SAMPLE COBOL PROGRAM.
>AUTHOR. SPENCER.
>DATE WRITTEN. FEBRUARY 20, 1974.
>DATE COMPLETED. FEBRUARY 21, 1974.
>REMARKS. SAMPLE PROGRAM COMPUTES AND
>   PRINTS THE PRODUCT OF 643 AND 746.
>ENVIRONMENT DIVISION.
>CONFIGURATION SECTION.
>SOURCE-COMPUTER. IBM-360.
>OBJECT-COMPUTER. IBM-360.
>DATA DIVISION.
>WORKING-STORAGE SECTION.
>77 NUMBER-ONE PICTURE 999 VALUE IS 643.
>77 NUMBER-TWO PICTURE 999 VALUE IS 746.

```
PROCEDURE DIVISION.
CALCULATION. COMPUTE TOTAL = NUMBER-ONE *
   NUMBER-TWO. DISPLAY TOTAL. STOP RUN.
END PROGRAM.
```

The Identification Division has five entries. The first entry gives the program a name. The next entry gives the programmer's name. The next two entries supply information about when the program was written and compiled. The last entry consists of a remark.

The Environment Division describes the type of computer to be used to compile and later run this program. The Data Division assigns English names to the numbers to be multiplied. The Procedure Division actually causes the computer to perform the computation and to print the answer.

Each line in these four divisions is keypunched on a separate punched card prior to submitting it to the computer for compilation and subsequent execution.

Finally, one statement in a COBOL program causes a series of machine language instructions to be set up and inserted at a particular point in the object program. This is true of all compiler language statements.

The PL/I Language

PL/I is a very general language with a wider scope than either FORTRAN or COBOL. At first glance, it gives the appearance of an extension of FORTRAN, with some commercial data processing features thrown in. Closer inspection discloses a language that, for all its extent, is unified and carefully designed.

Compared with FORTRAN, PL/I is both simpler to use and more powerful. There are fewer restrictions and fewer rules to learn. And yet, it offers many features which are not present in FORTRAN. PL/I notation is semiformal, like FORTRAN, rather than informal like English-based COBOL.

To illustrate the PL/I language, consider the following PL/I program for converting inches to centimeters (1 inch = 2.54 centimeters) for 12 values.

```
CVT: PROCEDURE OPTIONS (MAIN);
DECLARE (INCH) FIXED, (CENT) FIXED (10,12);
DO INCH = 1 BY 1 TO 12;
CENT = 2.54 * INCH;
PUT SKIP LIST (INCH, CENT);
END;
STOP;
END CVT;
```

This program, when compiled and executed on the computer, causes the following data to be printed:

1	2.54
2	5.08
3	7.62
4	10.16
5	12.70
6	15.24
7	17.78
8	20.32
9	22.86
10	25.40
11	27.94
12	30.48

The units in the left-hand column are understood to be inches, whereas those in the right-hand column are centimeters.

The APL Language

APL is a language for describing procedures in the processing of information. It can be used to describe mathematical procedures having nothing to do with computers, or to describe (to a human being) how a computer works. Most commonly, however, it is used for programming in the ordinary sense of directing computers how to process numerical or alphabetical data.

The language was invented by Dr. Kenneth E. Iverson and described in a book entitled *A Programming Language* (published by John Wiley & Sons in 1962).

APL is one of the most concise, consistent, and powerful programming languages ever devised. Operations on single items extend simply and naturally to arrays of any size and shape. Thus, for instance, a matrix addition that in other higher level languages (such as BASIC or FORTRAN) might require two loops and a half-dozen statements becomes simple A + B in APL.

The language is very mathematically oriented. It is, however, finding widespread acceptance among a variety of users, many of them in business and education.

The RPG Language

Report Program Generator (RPG) computer language provides a simple method for writing instructions for a computer to accomplish a variety of commercial data processing jobs. The purpose of RPG is simply to generate a report program. This program in turn is used to write the desired report.

RPG is used extensively in small-scale computer systems and is even finding acceptance in larger computer installations where there is a need for the production of business reports.

RPG is an easy language to learn and use. It is capable of handling several input files, selecting certain records from the files, performing limited mathematical computations, and producing the desired report from the records. During the process it can also update records from the master file.

The use of RPG is restricted to situations in which a simple report is desired from the computer rather than some complex processing or multiple output. It is a highly formalized language with very rigid specifications. Unlike other compiler languages in which instructions are given in RPG, the programmer need only furnish data and specify conditions and processing desired on special specification forms. Generally, four different types of specifications sheets are used in writing RPG programs. They specify (1) the form of input data, (2) the input-output devices to be used in executing the program, (3) the calculations that are required, and (4) the form of output data. A program specified on these special forms is translated by RPG into machine code instructions.

The BASIC Language

BASIC, an acronym for Beginner's All-purpose Symbolic Instruction Code, was developed at Dartmouth College in the late 1960s. Since BASIC is not only very easy to learn but also an ideal programming language for solving a variety of problems, it has been chosen for a more detailed discussion in the next chapter.

Questions

1. Define *programming.*
2. What is *machine language?*
3. What advantages does one gain by using a symbolic programming language?
4. What is a *translator?*
5. Distinguish between the following: (a) source program, (b) object program, (c) assembler program, and (d) compiler program.
6. What is the function of an *assembler?*
7. What is meant by the term, *high-level programming language?*
8. What is meant by the term, *compile-and-go?*
9. Discuss some general characteristics of compiler languages.
10. Name four compiler languages.
11. What is the function of a compiler?
12. Define *hardware* and *software.*

13. FORTRAN was designed primarily for solving data processing problems in banks and insurance companies. True or false?
14. The COBOL language (a) is used primarily for scientific applications, (b) is based on business English and is used in business applications, (c) is useful in translating foreign languages to machine language.
15. A PL/I compiler (a) complicates the programming process, (b) translates source language statements into machine language code, (c) is an input device used to read magnetic ink character documents.

8

Introduction to
Computer Programming

Introduction to the BASIC Programming Language

Ever since the first computer was invented, computer manufacturers, programmers, and computer users have been trying to find ways to simplify programming. Their aim has been to develop programming languages that are easy to understand, easy to learn, easy to use, and that are applicable to a large number of computers. One answer to this continuing effort is the BASIC programming language.

BASIC, which stands for Beginner's All-purpose Symbolic Instruction Code, is a programming language developed at Dartmouth College. It has been implemented on most microcomputers, minicomputers, time-sharing computer systems, and many medium and large-scale computers.

> **time-sharing computer system:** a system whereby more than one user may share the same computer by use of remote terminals.

The appeal of BASIC is its simplicity. A beginner who knows nothing about programming or computers can master the rudiments of BASIC in a few hours. Given a few more hours of practice at a terminal, the beginner will be pleasantly surprised to find that he can write programs for a variety of problems familiar to him. In a week's time, his confidence in his ability as a fledgling programmer will be readily confirmed.

BASIC is a language for the amateur programmer who

· Has a problem
· Wants to solve it easily, quickly, and conveniently

- Prefers to describe his own problems to a computer rather than to a programmer
- Has only modest amounts of input data to be used by the program.

BASIC permits a user to communicate his problem to a computer in a language composed of statements and equations. It permits him to define and solve programming problems rapidly.

Fundamentals of BASIC

A major reason why the BASIC language is easy to learn is that its vocabulary of statement types and symbols is limited. Unlike other languages, such as PL/I, FORTRAN, and COBOL, which have many rules and statement types, BASIC has no more than 20 or so different statements.

The statement is the core of the BASIC language. There are several fundamental types with differing functions:

- *Arithmetic statements,* which specify the mathematical operations that the computer must execute.
- *Program control statements,* which direct the sequence of operations in the program.
- *Input-output statements,* which describe the input-output operations needed to enter data and print results.

As we proceed through the chapter we shall discuss and illustrate each of these types of statements. Before we actually start to write programs with them, let us consider a couple of fundamental requirements:

- A line can contain only one statement.
- Every BASIC program must terminate with an END statement.
- Each statement must have a line number.
- Statements are executed by the computer in the order of their line numbers, not in the order of entry at the terminal.

Shown below is a complete BASIC program that will convert numbers in inches to ones in feet and inches and print a table of the converted numbers:

```
100   REM CONVERSION PROGRAM
110   READ I
120   LET F = INT(I/12)
130   LET A = I − F * 12
140   PRINT I, "INCHES EQUALS," F, "FEET", A, "INCHES"
150   GOTO 110
160   DATA 63,14,46,263,140
170   END
```

As seen in this example, a program consists of a sequence of statements. Each statement has a *line number,* a number between 1 and 99999, and begins on a new line. A program may contain *comments,* which are to be printed with the program but otherwise ignored. Each comment statement must start with the letters, REM.

> **comment:** a written remark which can be included in the coding of a program in order to clarify the procedures, but which have no effect on the computer itself. In BASIC, a comment must start with the letters, REM.

The Character Set

BASIC makes use of all letters of the alphabet (A through Z), all ten decimal digits (0,1,2, . . . 9), and the following special characters:

+	Plus	&	Ampersand
−	Minus	;	Semicolon
↑	Up arrow	:	Colon
/	Slash	'	Single quote
*	Asterisk	"	Double quote
(	Left Parenthesis	<	Less than
)	Right parenthesis	<=	Less than or equal to
	Blank	=	Equal to
,	Comma	>	Greater than
.	Period	>=	Greater than or equal to
		<>	Not equal to

Variables, Names, Values, and Constants

The fundamental quantities in BASIC are called *variables,* and these are identified by their *names.* Each variable represents a value that may be changed during the computation. A statement involving variables is always to be treated in the same way, regardless of the actual values which the variables may currently have. Some statements allow the current values of variables to be tested and thus determine subsequent action.

Names, which identify variables in BASIC, consist of a letter or a letter followed by a digit. Thus in the previous program, the variables were called I, A, and F.

> **variable:** a quantity which can assume numerical values.
> **name:** a value which identifies a variable, consisting in BASIC of a letter or a letter followed by a digit (for example, D6, A, or G3).

The following are *not* variables in **BASIC**, and for the reasons given:

    2S   (first character must be a letter and the second a digit)
  AB6 (only a single letter must be used)
  AR   (second character must be a digit)
  26   (first character must be a letter)
 A163 (only a single digit must be used)

When we say that "the value is N2" or that "there are K equations," we are really referring to the current value of the variable whose name is thereby given.

constant: data which remain unchanged in a program, for example, 126 or 143.2.

Numerical constants are written using the ordinary decimal notation. A scale factor (integral power of 10) may be included after the letter E.

integer: a whole number without a fractional part, for example, 408 is an integer, whereas 43.6 is not.
real number: a number with a decimal point, for example, 260.0, 63.7 or .0004.

Constants may be either *integers* or *real numbers,* with or without an exponent. An integer is a value that does not contain a fractional part or a decimal point. Real constants always include a decimal point and may or may not have a fractional part. Thus, 16428, and 1043 are integers; 16., 5.6, 15.16, and .281 are real numbers (without exponent); and 1.432E2 and 61.40E-3 are real numbers (with exponent). Moreover, 4.16, .416E1, 416.E-2, and .00416E3 are different ways of writing the same constant. In the example, .416E1, the *mantissa* is .416, 1 is the *exponent* (1 indicates 10 to the first power), and *E* simply means *with exponent.* Its mathematical equivalent is $.416 \times 10^1$, that is, 4.16. Similarly, the mathematic equivalent of 416.E-2 is 416×10^{-2}, that is, 4.16.

Commas must not appear in constants. For example, the number 74,162 would not be allowed. A negative constant *must* start with a minus ($-$) sign. A plus ($+$) sign for a positive number is optional. If a number is unsigned, it is assumed to be positive.

Fractions cannot be used directly, but must be written in decimal form. For example, the fraction 1 3/4 would be represented as 1.75.

Expressions

Several kinds of statements may contain *expressions,* which are written something like algebraic expressions and cause the current values of the specified elements to be combined in the specified ways. An element in an expression may be a variable, such as B8, or a constant, such as 2418.0.

The elements may be combined using the following arithmetic operators:

+   addition
−   subtraction
*   multiplication
/   division
↑   exponentiation

In some systems, two asterisks (**) are used in place of the arrow (↑).

expression: the symbolic representation of one or more operations, for example, A + B or P * Q.

The following are all valid expressions:

R + S − 16
A + 10
X * Y − 14 + 23

Expressions are evaluated according to the rules of precedence, whereby all operations of a higher precedence are performed before those of a lower precedence. When parentheses are used, the operations contained within parentheses are performed first. Operations of equal precedence are performed from left to right. In an expression with no parentheses, operations are evaluated in the following order:

1. *Exponentiation*
2. *Multiplication* or *division*
3. *Addition* or *subtraction.*

Two operation symbols must not be used in succession unless separated by parentheses. Thus the incorrect expression, X = Y * − Z, should be written X = Y * (−Z).

Mathematical expressions are converted to BASIC as follows:

Mathematical expression	Equivalent BASIC expression
$\dfrac{x + y}{a + b}$	(X + Y) / (A + B)
$ab - hy$	A * B − H * Y
$3x^2 + 2x - 3$	3 * X ↑ 2 + 2 * X − 3

$$\frac{a + b}{xy} \qquad\qquad (A + B) / (X * Y)$$

$$\left(\frac{1 - x}{1 + x}\right) \quad \left(\frac{v + 2}{v - 3}\right) \qquad\qquad (1 - X) * (V + 2) / ((1 + X) * (V - 2))$$

Let us now examine some BASIC statements and explore their applications.

LET Statement

The principal computational statement in BASIC is the LET statement, which has the general form,

$$\text{LET } v = x$$

where v is a variable and x is an expression. The equals symbol (=) in BASIC is not a mathematical equals sign; it means "is replaced by." Thus, this statement is interpreted to mean, "The value of the expression on the right of the *is replaced by* sign replaces the value of the variable on the left."

The LET statement in BASIC is very similar to the familiar arithmetic statement which is used in everyday mathematics. Some typical examples of the LET statement might be:

$$
\begin{array}{ll}
40 & \text{LET X = X + 1} \\
70 & \text{LET R = 14} \\
20 & \text{LET X = Y / 10 + 6}
\end{array}
$$

The statement, 40 LET X = X + 1, results in the value 1 being added to the value X in storage. The new sum replaces the original value of X. The statement, 70 LET R = 14, causes the number 14 to be assigned to R.

The LET statement may be used to set the variable to some starting value or to modify its value during a computation.

Reading and Writing

To do even a simple arithmetic problem, we need a way to get numbers into the computer and a method of printing the computed answer. One way to read data is to use the READ and DATA statements. Results may be printed by using a PRINT statement. For example, the program,

$$
\begin{array}{ll}
10 & \text{READ A, B, C} \\
20 & \text{LET X = A + B + C}
\end{array}
$$

```
30      PRINT X
40      DATA 9, 27, 18
50      END
```

would compute and print the sum of the numbers 9, 27, and 18. The READ statement directs the computer to go to the DATA list and read numbers from it. In this particular program, the computer is directed first to read the number 9 and assign it to A, then to read the number 27 and assign it to B, and finally to read the number 18 and assign it to C. (Notice the left-to-right sequence involved in these assignments.) The LET statement computes the sum of 9, 27, and 18 and assigns the sum to X. Then the PRINT statement prints the value of X.

There are several forms of the PRINT statement. Appearing alone, the word, PRINT, causes a line to be skipped on the printing device. The full statement,

PRINT "BASIC IS SIMPLE"

causes the message contained between quotation marks to be printed. A PRINT statement containing quotation marks is the only one in BASIC in which *blanks are counted*. The computer will print the message enclosed between quotation marks exactly. For example, the statement,

40 PRINT "CANDY IS SWEET"

will cause the three words enclosed in quotation marks to be printed with one space between each word. The statement,

60 PRINT "CANDY   IS   SWEET"

will cause four spaces to appear betwen the words, CANDY and IS, and seven spaces to appear between the words, IS and SWEET. In each case, the skipped spaces precisely match the skipped spaces in the statement.

Let us now examine how columns of data can be printed. Suppose that we have written a program to compute the electric power of several sets of values for resistance and current. Let's assume that our column headings are to be POWER, RESISTANCE, and CURRENT. To obtain these headings, we write:

20 PRINT "POWER", "RESISTANCE", "CURRENT"

To obtain the values, we write,

80 PRINT P, R, C

Thus the program,

```
20  PRINT "POWER", "RESISTANCE", "CURRENT"
30  PRINT
```

```
80   PRINT P, R, C
90   END
```

would cause a printed output similar to the following:

POWER	RESISTANCE	CURRENT
56.423	54.232	1.020
136.041	55.121	1.571
229.109	57.220	2.001
268.872	57.789	2.157
381.210	58.032	2.563

The *commas* contained in the **PRINT** statement caused the headings and values to be printed in specific column areas. The printout works on the following principle: The teletypewriter paper is divided horizontally into five 15-character zones, as shown below. When only one value is printed, as in a **PRINT X** statement, it is placed in Zone 1. When more than one value is printed, say **PRINT X,Y,Z**, the second value is placed in Zone 2, the third in Zone 3, and so forth. When more than five values are printed, the first five are placed in the five zones in order. The sixth value is printed on the next line in Zone 1, the seventh in Zone 2, and so forth. Whenever the quantity to be printed exceeds 15 characters, the printing continues into the next zone.

Columns on the teletypewriter paper	1-15	16-30	31-45	46-60	61-75
	Zone 1	Zone 2	Zone 3	Zone 4	Zone 5

Messages and variables can be mixed in the same **PRINT** statement. For example, the statement,

80   PRINT "GOLF =", G

will cause the *message,* GOLF =, to be printed in Zone 1, and the *value* of G to be printed in Zone 2. Thus if the current value of G was 27, then the following would be printed:

GOLF = 27

Let us now look at a **BASIC** program that uses the statements that we have discussed so far. Suppose that one wanted to compute the area of a flat ring that has an outside radius, R_1, of 8 inches and an inside radius, R_2, of 6 inches, as shown in the figure. The area is obtained by using the equation, AREA = $\pi (R_1{}^2 - R_2^2)$, in which π is the number 3.14159.

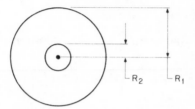

Computing area of a flat ring.

The following program would calculate the value of this equation for the variables given and when executed would print the area as 87.9645:

```
100   REM COMPUTE AREA OF RING
200   READ R1,R2
300   LET A = 3.14159 * (R1 ↑ 2 − R2 ↑ 2)
400   PRINT A
500   DATA 8,6
600   END
```

The last statement in the above program should now be explained. Every **BASIC** program *must* be terminated with an END statement. This statement must therefore have the highest-numbered line number in the program. It identifies the completion of the program just as the REM statement is used to give the program a title.

Program Control Statements

The sequence in which the computer executes statements is ordinarily determined by the order in which the statements are arranged. Thus far we have discussed only **BASIC** programs that are composed of statements to be executed in an unchanging sequence. Few problems suitable for computer processing, however, can be solved by a simple sequence of arithmetic statements. In many cases, the program will arrive at certain points at which it must decide where to go next on the basis of some condition it finds—for example, the condition of a number's being positive, zero, or negative. Depending on the outcome, the program either continues processing in a straight line order, branches to an earlier step in the program, skips to a later step in the program, or branches to an entirely different program sequence.

There are several statements in BASIC that allow the user to specify the sequence of program execution. Alternative program paths may depend on a specific condition at the time of execution. Line numbers serve as the markers by which program control statements can direct the sequence of the program.

The simplest statement for altering the sequence of execution is the GO-TO statement. Suppose, for example, that we wanted to compute values for Y in the equation,

$$Y = X^3 + 7X - 3$$

when X has the values 6, 12, 14, 9, 26, and 41. We could, of course, write the following lengthy program.

```
10  LET X = 6
15  LET Y = X ↑ 3 + 7 * X − 3
20  PRINT Y
25  LET X = 12
30  LET Y = X ↑ 3 + 7 * X − 3
35  PRINT Y
40  LET X = 14
45  LET Y = X ↑ 3 + 7 * X − 3
50  PRINT Y
55  LET X = 9
60  LET Y = X ↑ 3 + 7 * X − 3
65  PRINT Y
70  LET X = 26
75  LET Y = X ↑ 3 + 7 * X − 3
80  PRINT Y
85  LET X = 41
90  LET Y = X ↑ 3 + 7 * X − 3
95  PRINT Y
99  END
```

This program will certainly perform the required calculations, but if we make use of the GOTO statement, we can write a program that will produce the same result in 6 instead of 19 statements:

```
10  READ X
15  LET Y = X ↑ 3 + 7 * X − 3
20  PRINT Y
25  GO TO 10
30  DATA 6, 12, 14, 9, 26, 41
35  END
```

The above program computes and prints values for Y and keeps returning control to line number 10 until all data have been used.

To summarize, the GO TO statement consists of the words GO TO followed by a line number. When the computer encounters the GO TO statement, it causes program control to be transferred to the line number specified in the GO TO statement. Thus, if we said,

$$40 \quad \text{GO TO } 107$$

the computer would transfer control to the statement at line number 107, regardless of where line 107 might be in the program.

Often, one would like to transfer control to some statement in a program under some circumstances but not in others, depending on the results of intermediate calculations. This step is accomplished in BASIC by using the IF-THEN statement, which transfers control only if a certain condition is met.

The general form of the IF-THEN statement is as follows:

$$\text{IF e r e THEN ln}$$

where "e" is an expression, "ln" is a line number in the program, and "r" is one of the following relational operators:

Relational operator	Meaning
$<$	Less than
$<=$	Less than or equal to
$>$	Greater than
$>=$	Greater than or equal to
$=$	Equal to
$<>$	Not equal to

Suppose that one wanted to calculate the value of Y from the equation, $Y = 13X^2$, if the value of $A^2 - 2B^2$ is negative; otherwise, from the equation, $Y = 217X^3$. The program uses the following values: A = 28, B = 14, and X = 12.

```
100   REM TRANSFER OF CONTROL EXAMPLE
200   READ A, B, X
300   REM GO TO 700 IF A ↑ 2 − 2 * B ↑ 2 < 0
400   IF A ↑ 2 − 2 * B ↑ 2 < 0 THEN 700
500   LET Y = 217 * X ↑ 3
600   GO TO 800
700   LET Y = 13 * X ↑ 2
800   PRINT Y
900   DATA 28, 14, 12
999   END
```

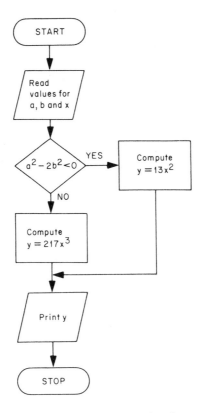

Flowchart for text example of transfer of control.

The program tests the value of the expression, $A^2 - 2B^2$, at statement 300. If the value is less than zero, then the next statement to be executed by the computer will be statement number 700, which computes the equation, $Y = 13X^2$. If the value of $A^2 - B^2$ is zero or greater, however, no transfer occurs at statement 300, and the next statement in the natural (sequential) order is executed. After Y is computed in statement 500, the GOTO in statement 600 causes control to pass directly to the PRINT statement, skipping the other calculation for Y.

Looping

One of the most important techniques in programming is the creation of *loops*. A loop consists of the repetition of a group of statements a number of times, usually with different values of one or more variables at each execution, until some specified condition is satisfied.

loop: a series of statements which are performed repeatedly until some specified condition is satisfied, whereupon a branch operation is obeyed to exit from the loop.

As shown in the previous section, loops can be written using the GOTO and IF-THEN statements. But, in BASIC a special statement is often more convenient for this purpose. The combination of the FOR and NEXT statements are used to create loops. A BASIC loop using these statements might appear as follows:

FOR K = 1 TO 200

. . . .   Statements

. . . .   that are

. . . .   repeated

. . . .   in the loop

NEXT K

The loop starts with the FOR statement and ends with the NEXT statement. This particular FOR statement instructs the computer to execute 200 times all the instructions between the FOR statement and the NEXT statement. In the first pass through the loop, the variable K is 1, in the second loop it is 2, in the third loop it is 3, and so on until K = 200 on the last loop.

The general form of the FOR statement is as follows:

$$\text{FOR } v = a \text{ TO } b \text{ STEP } c$$

where v is the *index,* a is the initial value of the index, b is the terminal value of the index, and c is the value by which the index is modified for each pass through the loop. Whenever the loop index is to be modified by 1 each time through the loop, that is, when c is equal to 1, the general form may be simplified to

$$\text{FOR } v = a \text{ TO } b$$

The general form of the NEXT statement is as follows:

$$\text{NEXT } v$$

where v is the same variable (used as an index) found in the corresponding FOR statement.

Let us do a sample program to illustrate the use of the FOR and the NEXT statements. The following program causes a table of values to be computed and printed. Note that all loop control information is contained in the one FOR statement: the index is X, the starting value is 1, the terminating value is 40, and since no step value is specified, the index increment is understood to be 1.

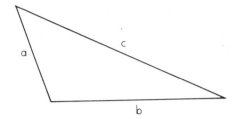

Computing area of a triangle.

```
100  REM TABULAR VALUES OF N
105  PRINT "X", "X2", "X3", "1/X", "SQUARE ROOT"
110  FOR X = 1 TO 40
115        LET X2 = X * X
120        LET X3 = X * X * X
125        LET R  = 1/X
130        LET S  = X ↑ .5
135        PRINT X, X2, X3, R, S
140  NEXT X
145  END
```

This program causes a 40-line table of values to be computed and printed. Note that all loop control information is contained in the one **FOR** statement: the index is **X**, the starting value is 1, the terminating value is 40, and since no step value is specified, the index increment is understood to be 1.

Let us now consider another looping example. Given the three sides of a triangle, a, b, and c, as shown in the figure, the area of the triangle can be calculated by the equation,

$$\text{Area} = \sqrt{s(s-a)(s-b)(s-c)}$$

where $s = (a + b + c)/2$.

The following program will compute the area for the two sets of data: a = 3, b = 4, c = 5 and a = 30, b = 20, c = 40.

```
10   REM COMPUTE AREA OF TRIANGLE
15   PRINT "A", "B", "C", "AREA"
20   FOR R = 1 TO 2
25        READ A, B, C
30        LET S = (A + B + C) / 2
35        LET A7 = (S*(S−A) * (S−B) * (S−C) ) ↑ .5
```

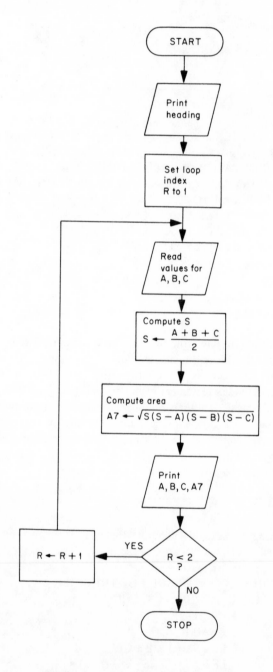

Flowchart for the area-of-triangle program.

```
40          PRINT A, B, C, A7
45  NEXT R
50  DATA 3, 4, 5
55  DATA 30, 20, 40
60  END
```

Keyboard Input during Computation

The user might prefer to supply the variables to be used in a BASIC program from the terminal keyboard during the actual execution of the program instead of specifying these values beforehand in a DATA statement. If he does, he might use a program similar to the one that follows:

```
20  PRINT "WHAT ARE THE VALUES FOR A, B, AND C"
40  INPUT A, B, C
60  LET S = A + B + C
80  PRINT "THE SUM IS", S
90  END
```

The first thing that this program would do is print the message,

> WHAT ARE THE VALUES FOR A, B, AND C
> ?

The INPUT statement causes a question mark to be printed on the line following the message. Whenever an INPUT statement is reached, the computer will pause and wait until the values for A, B, and C are typed by the person using the keyboard. When this is done, the program will resume computation and, assuming the person typed 300, 14, and 80, will give the following output, as specified by statement 80:

> THE SUM IS 394

The INPUT statement is ideally suited for use in programs that have two-way communications with the terminal user. For example, game programs, such as tic-tac-toe, nim, and blackjack, require the player to input each move or play. Another example is teaching programs that require responses from the student.

Library Functions

Very often when a program is being written, a situation arises that can easily be handled by a *library function.* BASIC includes the following library functions:

SQR(X)	Square root of X
SIN(X)	Sine of angle X
COS(X)	Cosine of angle X
TAN(X)	Tangent of X
ATN(X)	Arctangent of X
ABS(X)	Absolute value of X
EXP(X)	Exponent, e, to the power X
LOG(X)	Logarithm (base e) of X
INT(X)	Integer (whole number) part of X
SGN(X)	Algebraic sign of X
RND(X)	Random number

To use a library function in a program, one needs only to write the name of the function followed by parentheses enclosing the expression for which the function is to be computed.

library function: a facility in the BASIC language that performs a specific mathematical computation, for example, the square root of a number, the sine of an angle, etc.

For example, the following LET statement containing a square root library function,

$$60 \quad \text{LET A} = \text{SQR(R)}$$

will cause the square root of R to be computed and the result to be assigned to the variable A.

Several examples of mathematical expressions and their BASIC equivalents using library functions are shown below:

Mathematical expression	*BASIC expression*
$\sin(x + y)$	SIN (X + Y)
$\lvert x - 2 \rvert$	ABS (X − 2)
$a \cos \theta$	A * COS (T)
$\sqrt{a^2 + b^2 - 3}$	SQR (A ↑ 2 + B ↑ 2 − 3)

Random numbers can be generated very easily in BASIC by using the RND function, which produces six-digit random numbers.

Recurring Instruction Sets

In large programs, it often becomes necessary to execute a particular set of instructions several different times, at different points in the program. Rather than having to repeat this set of instructions each time it is to be executed,

BASIC provides two statements which allow the user to write just once the instruction set that is to be repeated. The GOSUB statement is used to transfer program control to the first instruction in the set that is to be used. The RETURN statement is used as the last instruction in the set that is to be used. To illustrate, let us consider the following program segment:

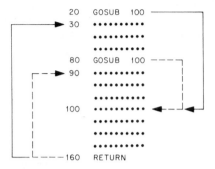

Statement 20 contains a GOSUB statement that will cause control to be transferred to statement 100, the first instruction in the set to be used. After executing the instructions following statement 100, statement 160 is encountered. This RETURN statement directs the computer to return control back to statement 30, the first statement after the one which transferred control to statement 100. A similar transfer and return operation would occur when statement 80 is executed. Here the RETURN statement at 160 would return control to statement 90.

Other Features of BASIC

This chapter did not present anything like a complete survey of BASIC, but a sufficient number of BASIC statements have been included to enable the reader to start writing programs and to solve problems on a computer. Readers interested in a more exhaustive treatment of the BASIC language are urged to read one of the BASIC texts listed at the end of this chapter. Some of the features of BASIC not yet discussed in this chapter will now be briefly identified.

BASIC includes a large set of matrix operations, which will be of most service for the more advanced user of the language. The matrix operations, which are specified by the MAT statement, include the following: the addition of two matrices, the subtraction of two matrices, the multiplication of two matrices, scalar multiplication, the inverse of a matrix, and several others.

matrix: a rectangular array of numbers that may be operated on using prescribed rules involving mathematical operations such as addition, subtraction, and the like.

BASIC also allows a user to define his own functions and give them names. The functions can then be used in a program by using the assigned name. This is accomplished by using the DEF statement.

The PRINT USING statement provides a convenient way of producing formatted output. The computed GOTO statement permits transfer of control to any one of a group of statements, with the particular one being chosen on the basis of results computed in the execution of the program. The RESTORE statement is used in conjunction with the READ and DATA statements and directs the computer to permit reading data again from the beginning of a DATA list. The STOP statement terminates the execution of a program. It serves the same purpose as a program transfer to the END statement.

BASIC provides the facility for working with one-dimensional *arrays* and two-dimensional *arrays* (also called *matrices*). The DIM statement is used to reserve computer storage for the placement of arrays.

Arrays: A series of related numerical items. An ordered arrangement or pattern of numbers, such as a list of numbers, a table of numbers, or a matrix.

Sample BASIC Programs

The beginning programmer, whether he is a high school student, college student, teacher, businessman, layman or scientist, is advised to start with problems that are relatively easy to understand. With a clear understanding of simple problems, he may gradually move on to more complicated problems. The reader should remember that there are often many possible approaches to any given problem.

The sample problems given here are written in a straightforward manner and contain comment statements to help the reader understand each program.

Accounting Problem

The Widget Manufacturing Company wishes to use BASIC to solve a simple accounting problem. A welding machine worth $9,000 is to be depreciated over 20 years by the use of a double declining-balance depreciation. The following program was written by one of their accountants from the flowchart shown:

```
100   REM ACCOUNTING PROBLEM
120   PRINT "YEAR", "DEPRECIATION", "BOOK VALUE"
140   LET C = 9000
160   LET L = 20
```

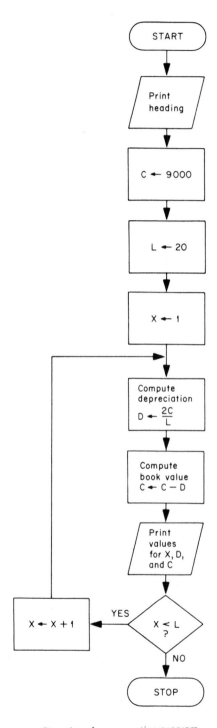

Flowchart for accounting program.

```
180   FOR X = 1 TO L
200         REM COMPUTE DEPRECIATION
220         LET D = 2 * C/L
240         REM COMPUTE BOOK VALUE
260         LET C = C - D
280         REM PRINT X,D, AND C
300         PRINT X, D, C
320   NEXT X
340   END
```

Statement 120 causes three headings to be printed by the teletypewriter. Statements 140 and 160 cause the variables C and L to be set to 9000 and 20, respectively. The variable C represents the original value of the machine, and L represents the number of years over which its value is to be depreciated. Statements 180 through 320 determine the depreciated and book value for each year, printing the values as they are calculated. Statements 100, 200, 240, and 280 are placed in the program to supply supplementary comments (or REMs).

This program produced the following output:

YEAR	DEPRECIATION	BOOK VALUE
1	900	8100
2	810	7290
3	729	6561
4	656.1	5904.9
5	590.49	5314.41
6	531.441	4782.97
7	478.297	4304.67
8	430.467	3874.2
9	387.42	3486.78
10	348.678	3138.11
11	313.811	2824.3
12	282.43	2541.87
13	254.187	2287.68
14	228.768	2058.91
15	205.891	1853.02
16	185.302	1667.72
17	166.772	1500.95
18	150.095	1350.85
19	135.085	1215.77
20	121.577	1094.19

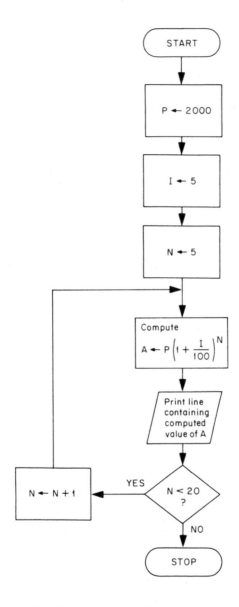

Flowchart for compound interest program.

Compound Interest Problem

The formula used for computing compound interest is as follows:

$$A = P \left(1 + \frac{I}{100}\right)^n$$

where P is the principal (the amount originally invested or deposited), I is the yearly rate of interest, n is the number of years, and A is the amount (principal + interest). The following program, coded from the flowchart shown, computes the values of an initial deposit of $2000 invested at 5 percent interest for 5 to 20 years.

```
100   REM COMPOUND INTEREST PROBLEM
200   LET P = 2000
300   LET I = 5
400   REM CALCULATE VALUES FOR 5–20 YEARS
500   FOR N = 5 TO 20
600          LET A = P * (1 + I / 100) ↑ N
700          PRINT "IN"; N; "YEARS, THE AMOUNT WILL BE"; A
800   NEXT N
900   END
```

This program illustrates a simple loop. Statements 200, 300, and 900 are executed only once, whereas statements 500, 600, 700, and 800 are executed 16 times (for N = 5,6,7, . . . ,20). REM statements 100 and 400, which are not executed, appear in the program as supplementary information. In statement 700, semicolons are used instead of commas so that the printed entities will appear side-by-side instead of in separate zones.

The output of this program is as follows:

```
IN 5 YEARS, THE AMOUNT WILL BE 2552.56
IN 6 YEARS, THE AMOUNT WILL BE 2680.19
IN 7 YEARS, THE AMOUNT WILL BE 2814.2
IN 8 YEARS, THE AMOUNT WILL BE 2954.91
IN 9 YEARS, THE AMOUNT WILL BE 3102.66
IN 10 YEARS, THE AMOUNT WILL BE 3257.79
IN 11 YEARS, THE AMOUNT WILL BE 3420.68
IN 12 YEARS, THE AMOUNT WILL BE 3591.71
IN 13 YEARS, THE AMOUNT WILL BE 3771.3
IN 14 YEARS, THE AMOUNT WILL BE 3959.86
IN 15 YEARS, THE AMOUNT WILL BE 4157.86
IN 16 YEARS, THE AMOUNT WILL BE 4365.75
IN 17 YEARS, THE AMOUNT WILL BE 4584.04
```

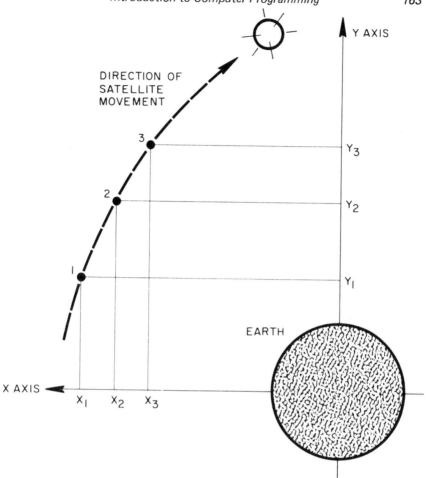

Path of a satellite in terms of an X-Y coordinate system fixed to the center of the earth.

IN 18 YEARS, THE AMOUNT WILL BE 4813.24
IN 19 YEARS, THE AMOUNT WILL BE 5053.9
IN 20 YEARS, THE AMOUNT WILL BE 5306.6

Satellite Orbit Problem

The illustration shows the path of a satellite and an X–Y coordinate system fixed to the center of the earth. The points labeled 1, 2, and 3 specify the positions of the satellite at equal time intervals, that is, the satellite requires the same time to move from Position 2 to Position 3 as from Position 1 to

Position 2. The coordinates of Position 3 can be computed if the coordinates of Positions 1 and 2 are known. This computation is accomplished by the following two equations:

$$X_3 = 2X_2 + X_1 \left(\frac{C}{(X_1^2 + Y_1^2)^{3/2}} \right) - 1$$

$$Y_3 = 2Y_2 + Y_1 \left(\frac{C}{(X_1^2 + Y_1^2)^{3/2}} \right) - 1$$

where C is a constant that is determined by the gravitational attraction of the earth for the satellite and the time interval previously discussed. Computation of Position 3 allows any number of points, N, to be computed from the two preceding points.

The following program, coded from the flowchart shown, reads in values for N, C, and the coordinates for the first two points, and it then computes the coordinates of N additional points. The computed points determine the orbit of the satellite.

```
100   REM SATELLITE ORBIT PROBLEM
120   PRINT "TYPE VALUES FOR N, C, X1, Y1, X2, Y2";
140   INPUT N, C, X1, Y1, X2, Y2
160   PRINT
180   PRINT "COORDINATES OF SATELLITE ORBIT"
200   PRINT
220   PRINT "POINT NUMBER", "X COORDINATE", "Y COORDINATE"
240   PRINT
260   PRINT " 1", X1, Y1
280   PRINT " 2", X2, Y2
300   FOR K = 1 TO N
320         LET X3 = 2 * X2 + X1 * (C/((X1↑2+Y1↑2) ↑ 1.5) −1
340         LET Y3 = 2 * Y2 + Y1 * (C/((X1↑2+Y1↑2) ↑ 1.5) −1
360         PRINT K+2, X3, Y3
380         LET X1 = X2
400         LET X2 = X3
420         LET Y1 = Y2
440         LET Y2 = Y3
460   NEXT K
480   END
```

Statement 120 causes a message to be printed by the teletypewriter. Statement 140 is used to input the coordinates of the first two points, X1, Y1, and X2, Y2, as well as the number of points to be computed by the program, N, and the constant, C. The next five statements cause a table heading to be

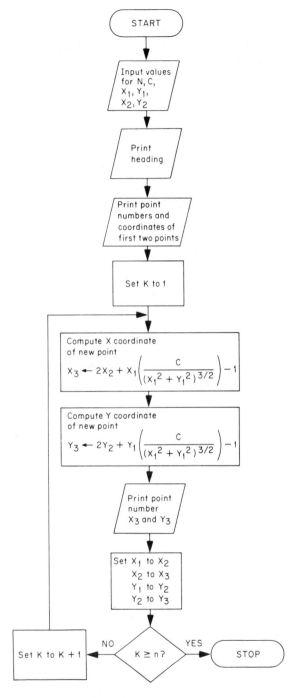

Flowchart for satellite orbit program.

printed by the teletypewriter. Statements 260 and 280 cause the first two lines
of table data to be printed.

Statements 300 and 460 set up a loop that is repeated N times. Each time
through the loop the coordinates for a new point are computed and printed by
statements 320, 340, and 360. Statements 380 through 440 are used to update
the variables X1, X2, Y1, and Y2 for use in computations during the next pass
through the program loop. The END statement terminates the program. The
program produces the following output:

TYPE VALUES FOR N, C, X1, Y1, X2, Y2? 10, 1000, 103, 64, 94, 81

COORDINATES OF SATELLITE ORBIT

POINT NUMBER	X COORDINATE	Y COORDINATE
1	103	64
2	94	81
3	85.0578	98.0359
4	76.1647	115.114
5	67.3106	132.237
6	58.4854	149.404
7	49.6808	166.612
8	40.8904	183.855
9	32.1095	201.13
10	23.3346	218.433
11	14.5636	235.76
12	5.79475	253.107

Questions

1. What are some advantages to using a programming language such as **BASIC**?
2. Which of the following are invalid variables in **BASIC** and why? (a) XY, (b)
   B2, (c) 68, (d) A, (e) 7D, (f) R∗.
3. What is the REM statement used for?
4. Specify the precedence of the five **BASIC** arithmetic operations.
5. Which arithmetic operation would be performed first in the following
   expression: $X + Y * R$?
6. In this expression, what arithmetic operation should be done first: $(A + B)$
   ↑ 2?
7. Rewrite any of the following expressions that would be incorrect in
   BASIC: (a) $A + B^2$, (b) $A + BC + D$, and (c) $A * B + C \times D$.
8. Write **BASIC LET** statements to represent the following algebraic expressions: (a) $x = (a + b - c)d$, (b) $r = (x + y)^{1/2}$, (c) $s = (a + b)/r$.

9. How many values will be read by the following statement: 20 READ A,B,C,X1,X2,Y?

10. Write a statement to print the message: THE NEW MACHINES.

11. Draw a flowchart that could be used to write this BASIC program:

```
100  READ A
200  LET B =3
300  LET C = 12/B
400  LET S = A + B + C
500  PRINT S
600  DATA 27
700  END
```

12. Write a BASIC program that will read values for A, B, and C and print them, first in the order read and then in reverse order.

13. Write a BASIC program to find out if X is between −40 and +40. If X falls within these limits, the computer is to print out TRUE; if not, FALSE.

14. Write a BASIC program to produce a multiplication table for all numbers up to and including 10.

15. In the following program, what is the final value of R?

```
10  LET R = 3
20  FOR J = 1 TO 14
30      IF R < J THEN 50
40      LET R = R + 1
50  NEXT J
60  END
```

16. Write a program to compute the square and cube values of the first 15 integers. The program should produce a printout in the following form:

N	SQUARE	CUBE
1	1	1
2	4	8
3	9	27
.	.	.
.	.	.
.	.	.

17. The average temperature for six given months in Atlanta, Georgia are as follows: June, 86; July, 91; August, 95; December, 57; January, 52; February, 51. Write a BASIC program that will compute the average summer and winter temperatures in Atlanta. After the values have been computed, the program is to print the two following messages and the

values that complete them: (1) AVERAGE SUMMER TEMPERATURE IN ATLANTA IS, and (2) AVERAGE WINTER TEMPERATURE IN ATLANTA IS.

18. Write a program that will compute the batting average of the following five players and print a table of information in the order of decreasing batting average. The necessary data are given in the following table:

Player Number	Times at Bat	Hits
1	118	37
2	107	31
3	98	40
4	114	26
5	202	42

Batting average is computed by the formula,

$$\text{Batting average} = \frac{1{,}000 \times \text{hits}}{\text{Times at bat}}$$

Index

Abacus, 20-21
Access time, 89
Address, storage, 89
Aiken, Howard, 28-30
Aldrin, Edwin, 10
Altair 8800, 11, 38, 40
Analog computer, 43-44
Analytical Engine, 23-25
APL, 5, 129, 137
Applications, 8-16
Arithmetic unit, 46
Arithmometer, 25
Armstrong, Neil, 10
Array, 158
Assembler, 127
Assembler language, 121, 126-127
Atanasoff, John V., 30
Audio response unit, 81-82
Automatic programming, 127-128
Automatic Sequence Controlled
    Calculator, 27-30

Babbage, Charles, 23-25
Baldwin, Frank Stephen, 25-26
BASIC, 5, 129, 137-138, 140-166
    arrays, 158
    character set, 142
    comments, 142
    constants, 142-143
    expressions, 143-145
    fundamentals of, 141-142
    keyboard input, 155
    library functions, 155-156
    looping in, 151-152
    names, 142-143

BASIC *(continued)*
    program control statements, 148-155
    programs. *See* BASIC programs, sample
    reading in, 145-148
    statements. *See* BASIC statements
    variables, 142-143
    writing in, 145-148
BASIC programs, sample
    accounting, 158-160
    area of a ring, 148
    area of a triangle, 153-155
    compound interest, 161-163
    computational, 153
    number conversion, 141
    satellite orbit, 163-166
BASIC statements
    DATA, 145
    DIM, 158
    END, 148
    FOR, 152
    GO TO, 149-150
    GOSUB, 157
    IF-THEN, 150
    INPUT, 155
    LET, 145
    MAT, 157
    NEXT, 152
    PRINT, 146-148
    PRINT USING, 158
    READ, 145
    REM, 142
    RESTORE, 158
    RETURN, 157
    STOP, 158
Binary, 31, 123-124
Bit, 59

169